T0130204

the rain
that
never stops

AND THE PROBLEM OF DEPRESSION

m.r. scott

WESTBOW
PRESS®
A DIVISION OF THOMAS NELSON
& ZONDERVAN

WestBow Press books may be ordered through booksellers or by contacting:

WestBow Press
A Division of Thomas Nelson & Zondervan
1663 Liberty Drive
Bloomington, IN 47403
www.westbowpress.com
844-714-3454

ISBN: 978-1-6642-8186-8 (sc)
ISBN: 978-1-6642-8187-5 (hc)
ISBN: 978-1-6642-8185-1 (e)

Library of Congress Control Number: 2022919667

Print information available on the last page.

WestBow Press rev. date: 10/31/2022

I want to dedicate this book to my late mentor and former pastor who lived his life for the glory of Jesus Christ, and also to my wife, who has always supported my writing and encouraged me, even when I doubted myself.

the rain that *never* stops

i looked out my window to see
the first cloud of gray approaching
to steal away the sun
before the pouring began
of a rain that never stops;
i couldn't find a reason
nor grasp its hidden worth
so i went to close the curtain
but upon seeing the flower, i knew.

CONTENTS

1

I Looked Out My Window To See

It's said that from beginning to end, the creation and setting of a stage for a play can take weeks or even months to complete. The play itself, of course, is far shorter than the time it took to create it. I find it fascinating that such time and energy can be invested into theater—over the course of what can be considered significant time—for an event that only lasts a fraction as long as its own creation. Generally speaking, people go to these plays to observe and interact with the characters—the drama. They may admire the settings, the stage, and the display, but it is not the focal point of why they are there. It is, both literally and figuratively, just a background after all. The real thrust of their attendance to such events is to partake in what unravels on that stage. Because of this, the production team does not preface their work with a laborious explanation of why they choose green drapes, or why the main character is wearing a purple tunic instead of a brown one. Indeed, it would be painful to sit through hours and hours rehashing the decisions and their motivations. For that reason, though I must preface this work with an explanation of why and how it came to be, I will do my best not to bore you with all the irrelevant details (and certainly won't take weeks to set up the chapter for you)!

The foundation of this work is heavily based upon my own experience with the problem of depression. I find that my most influential and meaningful work stems from my own experiences with the subjects and depression is no exception. As I go about my life, it would appear to be that I am not the only one fighting with this monster. Many persons I know have a familiarity with depression, if only having suffered it for a season. Others have hinted at suffering it, while a few have outright told me that they are in one way or another engaged in a fierce battle where swords are swung, and flesh is ripped to pieces. It comes as no surprise that depression has such a far reach, nor does it surprise me that as many people struggle with it as they do despite the overwhelming number of self-help and positive "you can do better" books flooding the shelves of our local bookstores. It seems like the world's answer is within the grasp of our fingers, yet the answer has never seemed so far away. But why is the problem of depression so pervasive that we can't seem to shake it no matter what we do?

To be sure, the problem of depression is not one easily solved. It is a burden, and a complex one at that, especially since the root of it can reach further back into our pasts than we might be aware of. For some, their depression is rooted in a trauma they experienced in their lifetime. This could come in the form of abandonment, abuse, the death of a loved one, the loss of a job or spouse, or something else. Others have no discernible trauma, but rather have chemical imbalances in the brain. Many others suffer from depression that is the result of spiritual drought. Some depression is temporary, while other forms are chronic. Some depression manifests with relatively low impact, while others drown the soul. One of the puzzling obstacles about solving depression is while it seems simple on the surface, it has complexities and variables that all need to be taken into consideration before attempting to tackle it head on.

While the aim of this work is to point the reader to freedom from the burden of depression, it must be understood that the scope of this work leans more toward anecdotal as opposed to academic. I am not licensed to diagnose or treat depression. I am not a psychiatrist, but I am a human intimately familiar with the problem of depression, having battled with it for the last fourteen or so years. Because of this, I feel that I can make this work relatable to those who are in the same trench as I am, even if they're a few feet down the way. Sometimes, one of the uncanny aids to our most desperate battle is realizing that we are not alone, that there are others like us, and that we need not be ashamed of our burdens. While I do not discredit modern medicine and have found great help in utilizing counseling for myself, I recognize that the availability of those resources may be outside the reach of some. However, I believe in the efficacy of this work in providing clear perspective to those who take up and read it. It is also pertinent to state here that if you have thoughts or temptations to hurt yourself or worse, it is best for you to seek prompt help. Regardless of where you go, however, be sure to keep this book with you.

Most people who meet me for the first time soon come to know that I'm a Christian and that my relationship to Christ as my Lord defines all that I am and the way I see the world. I will go into more detail about that in the proceeding chapters, but for now, it will suffice to say that just because this book has a theological framework does not mean that the book cannot serve its purpose in helping you in your battle. I will say with all humility that there is no hope in this world outside of Christ and no life to be found in death. I will endeavor to show it in this work as I bear my soul and pour out all that I have in hopes that God's mercy breaks through your heart—and no, this is not a prosperity message. This is not a work claiming that if you believe in Jesus, your battle with depression ends and your experiences of suffering are over. To make such a grandiose claim would be to err greatly, both in my integrity and in representing the Word of God. We live in a world marred by sin, overrun with brokenness, and destitute of God in a great majority of places and governments. If God is life, then the absence of His presence can only be death. Because this work is theological in nature, I will be drawing my sources from the Scriptures. Truly, it is no exaggeration for me to proclaim that Christ is the only reason that I am still here and the reason why I write this work. It is a testimony to His grace, love, and compassion; a call to arms for my fellow believers to get in the trenches; and a beacon of hope to those who do not yet know Christ as Lord and Savior.

So as you take up and read, I encourage you to remember that you are not alone, that there is hope, and it is found in Christ, who will by no means turn you away if you come to Him in faith. May this work bless you, whether a believer or not, and may the Lord be glorified by the words on these pages.

2

The First Cloud of Gray Approaching

I *don't want to be here anymore.*
If I was looking in a mirror at the genesis of this thought, I am sure that my expression would have been one of confusion. I was standing in the family den when all of a sudden, this thought sprung into my mind. I gazed out the window. It was winter, and while I don't remember if there was any snow, I do remember that it was bleak. Gray.

Standing there alone, I felt a bit unsettled that I would think something like that. I had always been taught that suicide was bad. Yet, what made the thought worse was that it was followed by a desire to hurt myself—to take myself away from the gray of the world. I imagined myself going into the kitchen, grabbing a knife from the drawer, and running it across my wrists. I wondered what my mother's expression would be when she found my corpse, or if my brother would have regretted the way he had treated me all my life. I also wondered if anyone would truly care. I kept thinking to myself, *Why not?*

They say that isolation is a dangerous thing for humans because, by nature, we're relational beings. In that den, I was alone because in that house I was alone. There was no noise except that of my buzzing thoughts and *The Office* playing across the television screen. In that loneliness, I tried to piece together why I would feel that way. I quickly surmised that I was simply flirting with taboo thoughts because I knew that I wasn't supposed to think them. So I dismissed it, though from that moment on, the depression would only continue to grow.

As time crept by, I felt as though the world was continuing to lose its luster. Color seemed to wash out. My world began to feel increasingly gray. To make matters worse, life's burdens would by no means alleviate the depression I was experiencing. One bad moment had the potential to obliterate the ten good moments that preceded it. In some respects, I became internally cold. I felt indifferent toward a lot of different things, especially my outer family issues with my immediate family. There was always some sort of conflict. I recall one time when I was at my grandmother's house downstairs in the basement. Attached to the house was a sunroom that acted like a porch. In the cool of the night, my cousin asked me about how I felt about the family situation and if I missed anyone. She asked that second question because when family conflict would arise, it was inevitable that the family would no longer associate for a time. The drama of the adults quickly trickled into the lives of the children.

I thought about it for a fraction of a second before I told my cousin that it never bothered me not to see the family. I rarely missed people. My cousin looked at me and to my surprise, said, "Wow, M.R., you've gotten really cold." A comment like that today would cause me to self-analyze. A comment like that then? I didn't flinch. There was no impact. To me, they were just words.

This is not to say that I was a recluse, or emotionally detached from the world. Ironically enough, I have always possessed a relatively keen empathy. I relate well to others and their emotions. I spent much time talking my peers through relational issues, felt very powerful emotions in other ways, but nothing as strong or fortuitous as my depression. It had a tenacity that could give Hercules an inferiority complex.

In a lot of ways, my depression has shaped me into the man I am. While I will share more about this in the proceeding chapters, it will suffice to say for now that the depression you now suffer is not in vain, nor is it purposeless. To be sure, nothing in this universe is. But what is depression truly?

"Depression? Isn't that just a fancy word for feeling 'bummed out'?" is what Dwight Schrute says to his boss, Michael Scott, when Michael is putting on a display of the dangers of depression by pretending that he is going to throw himself off the roof of the company building.

After calling Dwight a pejorative, Michael goes on to assert that, "Depression is a very serious illness."

Michael's response, while not exactly proper as far as a theological perspective is concerned, is right about depression being a very serious illness. The reality is, many people associate depression with simply being sad, but it is far worse, and anyone can tell you that depression is more akin to despair and hollowness than it is about feelings of sadness. We know that intense moments of grief and/or trauma can cause seasonal depression, where the response of the grief or trauma is so elevated that its symptoms often mock depression. We also know that certain life changes can prompt such responses as well, such as women who suffer postpartum depression. Before diving into some of these topics, however, I want to state a few things.

First, there is no shame in suffering from depression. The truth of the matter is sin has marred the entirety of creation. In the Garden of Eden, Adam, the first created human, had paradise. God gives Adam a woman, whom he calls Eve, and both live in the garden enjoying the paradise that God made for them. However, shortly after describing creation, the narrative of Adam and Eve takes a sinister turn when Satan, in the guise of a serpent, deceives Eve, and influences her to disobey God's only command not to eat from the tree of the knowledge of good and evil. This disobedience was completed when Eve gave Adam and fruit, and he ate of it as well. It is important to keep this in mind, as the result of that wickedness has reaped consequences for us all. The consequences of sin are so severe, in fact, that Paul writes that the entirety of creation groans for redemption (see Romans 8:19–23).

In order for this to make sense, we have to summarize what sin is. In brief, sin is a want of God's righteousness, or a want of conformity to the law of God. At this juncture, you may be scratching your head wondering, "How is a wanting to conform to God's law sin? Isn't sin supposed to be a bad thing?" You would be correct if we were using the modern understanding of "want" as being that which relates to desire. However, there is another usage of the word want, and it means *lack of*. So in a very real sense, sin is a lack of God's righteousness, and a lack of conformity to God's law.

To understand what a lack of God's righteousness means, we have to first know what it is that God is in His nature and His character. I add God's character because God's character is supremely relevant, for we are made in God's image.[1] For example, the Bible teaches us that God is truth, life, and light (see John 1:1–5; 14:6). What would the lack of those characteristics look like? Deception, death, and darkness. Ours is a society that rejects God. If God is light, then by process of elimination, to run from Him is to run into the dark. Another attribute of God is that God is orderly. A lack of order is unmitigated chaos. When we run away from God, these are the things that we must run toward.[2]

So, coming back to Adam and Eve, when they disobeyed the Creator, they subjected themselves and creation to futility, and along with it, us. This is because by nature, Adam and Eve were sinners, and two sinners who procreate cannot make something outside of their natures, thus, another sinner is born. The more sinners that enter the world, the worse it gets, until God destroys the world through the flood,

---

[1] Here, the word "image" does not refer to physical attributes that are shared between man and God. Rather, it refers to the attributes of God that are communicated, or shared, with man. Such attributes, called the communicable attributes of God, include attributes such as volition, sentience, emotion, and spiritual and moral awareness. Man has the capacity for love because God is love (1 John 4:16).

[2] Another way to look at this is to contrast light and darkness. We know that light has substance and darkness is a lack of light. When we turn a light on, we are not turning the darkness off, and vice versa, when we turn a light off, we are not turning the darkness on. In an analogous manner, sin is a lack of God's righteousness.

save Noah and his family. Why didn't God destroy Noah too? We will answer that later on in the book.

If a broken world is where we live and all of us are broken, then is it any surprise that brokenness resides within us? That our emotions, our thoughts, our relationships, our perceptions are broken? If this is the case—and it certainly is—then the experiencing of depression or sorrow of any kind is not something to be ashamed of. In fact, Solomon writes in Ecclesiastes, **It is better to go to the house of mourning than to go to the house of feasting, for this is the end of all mankind, and the living will lay it to heart** (7:2). We read of Jesus that He wept at the death of Lazarus and the sorrow of the crowds (see John 11), and that He prayed and cried to God (Hebrews 5:7). Many characters recorded for us in Scripture also suffered with bouts of depression, some even asking God to take their lives!

The second thing I want you to know is that God is sovereign over all things, including your depression. Many people, when discussing the problem of evil as it relates to God's sovereignty get it wrong. To be sure, their intentions are generally good. They wish to absolve God of all possible involvement with the evils and sufferings of this world. They will make statements like, "This suffering isn't God's will for your life!" and, "You just have to have faith and God will heal you!" or, "God has nothing to do with the evil in this world!" Such statements, while again, having good intentions, are not biblical. Why do I say this?

Scripture is rather clear that God is sovereign over all things. This includes the problem of evil. In Isaiah 45:7, we read what appears to be a problematic text: **I form the light and create darkness; I make well-being and create calamity. I am the LORD who does all these things.** That is God speaking. A lot of critics point out this text in contrast with James 1:13, **Let no one say when he is tempted, "I am being tempted by God," for God cannot be tempted with evil, and He Himself tempts no one.** Here, James clearly asserts that God does not create evil or tempt mankind with evil. Yet Isaiah tells us that God creates evil. Is this a contradiction?

Not exactly. In Hebrew literature, one of the main devices to stress a point is to engage in parallelism. A parallelism is when two statements are side-by-side, or successive, to demonstrate a point. There are three types of parallelisms: synonymous, antithetical, and synthetic. Each type involves communicating a singular message. In Isaiah 45:7, we get the Lord speaking to us by way of antithetical parallelism to illustrate His absolute sovereignty over all things. It is not as though God sits up in heaven, creates little balls of evil, and tosses them down into earth, but rather, it is to say that both goodness and evil fall under the scope of God's authority. Remember, evil, like darkness, is a lack of something. God does not create evil—evil comes about by the deprivation of God, which in our natural, sinful state, we all suffer.

Many people become aghast when I tell them that their suffering—including their and my depression—is under God's authority. In His wisdom, God decreed it to pass that I would battle with this malady. He has also decreed it in yours, if you so suffer. People often scoff at such a remark, saying that makes God a tyrant. One question ought to be enough to make us stop and realize what a fool's errand it is to try to rip anything out of the hands of God. The question is this: *if God is not sovereign over evil, then where did it come from, and who is?* A myriad of questions can then be derived from that question: (1) *If God is not sovereign over the evil in this world, does that mean that He wants to stop it but cannot, or that He could stop it but does not want to?* (2) *If evil is a force that exists outside the control and sovereignty of God, then does that mean it could thwart God?* (3) *If evil is not in the control of God, then what is its purpose?*

The list goes on. If there is no God, then our suffering is indifferent in an indifferent universe, and there is no objective purpose to it other than the purpose we assign it ourselves. That makes its purpose meaningless and subjective.

The truth is, God is Lord over life and death, and has, in His perfect wisdom, so ordered the universe to include the fall of man and subsequent consequences of sin, death, and evil. Scripture is clear that the purpose of all things is the glory of God in Christ and that part of this is the redemption of the creation by virtue of what Christ accomplishes on the cross. We will get into this more in the final chapter.

I could not imagine wanting my depression in anyone else's hands but God's. I could not imagine wanting a world where evil acts independently of God's sovereignty, where God is powerless to stop it. To be sure, if my suffering and depression are in the hands of God, then I can know immediately that my suffering—severe as it may be—is not in vain. In other words, my hope has not been taken.

Thirdly, our suffering in this life is often the oil that causes the lanterns of our faith to burn the brightest if we are trusting God with it. Whether you can believe it or not, if you trust in Christ, what you find to be your greatest detriment, God will use to His greatest glory and your greatest good. How can I say this? When I look over the course of my life thus far, it is clear to me that the charity and joy of my life has been elevated greatly by the depression I suffer. I know the unplumbed depths of my depression. I also am aware that others in this life may be feeling the same way as I do yet without the ability to share it or ask for help. Because of this, I don't want people to feel the same way I do. I don't wish for them to experience the despondency of sorrow, the constant internal questioning, and the wondering of why they're here. So I strive to be a burst of energy, positivity, and joy. In other words, I strive to live out the light and life Christ has given me. Those who understand depression realize that it's not something to be wished upon anyone.

Because of this, I believe my empathy and my ability to meet people where they are, have been increased. I can pick up on subtle cues that people give off, even if they do so subconsciously. For a brief example, once, while at work, I noticed one of the young ladies seemed off. I simply checked in with her and let her know that if she needed anything, that I would be there to talk to. Two days later she approaches me with a big smile and thanks me. At that point in time, I had no idea why she was thanking me. She went on to explain that on the night I had asked her if everything was okay, she was planning to commit suicide. When I checked in, it was the push she needed to seek help because she saw that someone cared about her, even if in such a small way. Without my depression, I could have missed those subtleties, or could have been indifferent to someone else's plight, causing me to overlook them. So even though it may feel like your depression is a curse simply to be wished away, don't miss the silver lining. Things that are broken and useless to us do not limit the way that God can use them for our good and His glory.

Fourth, depression is not a battle meant to be fought alone. Isolation is the worst thing for a person suffering depression, which is ironic given the fact that depression causes us to self-isolate. When I lived in Phoenix for a year, it was one of the worst years of my life. I was battling severe depression every day. My anxieties and guilt feelings ran rampant for different reasons. I stopped going to church, I dove into sin to numb the pain, and I was all the worse for it. Why is isolation such a terrible idea?

Perhaps the most pressing reason to avoid isolation is that depression is a spiritual warfare as much as it is a mental one. There is a certain someone who would love for nothing more than for you to isolate away from your loved ones and from God, and if you aren't a believer, even better for him. I'm talking about Satan. Peter describes Satan in this way: **Be sober-minded; be watchful. Your adversary the devil prowls around like a roaring lion, seeking someone to devour** (1 Peter 5:8). This imagery is stark as much as it is clear: lions thrive on prey that is alone. Lions also generally only go for prey within its ability to kill. And take note of the language Peter uses—the devil is looking for someone to devour, or to kill. If you isolate yourself, you are under attack by at least two sources: your own sinful flesh and the forces of Satan.

One might ask how Peter came away with this kind of imagery. It may have something to do with a conversation that Peter had with Jesus shortly before Jesus's betrayal. Jesus tells Peter, **"Simon, Simon, behold, Satan wished to have you, that he might sift you like wheat"** (22:31). In this, Jesus informs Peter that Satan was coming like a whirlwind, desiring to take Peter and destroy him, which, Jesus remarks, would be simple for Satan to do. However, Jesus continues: **"but I have prayed for you that your faith may not fail. And when you have turned again, strengthen your brothers"** (v. 32). Had Jesus not prayed for Peter, Peter would have been ground into dust. For those of us outside of God's protection, we are mere mice in the lion's jaw, and his intention is to kill.[3] Therefore, nothing delights Satan than when we isolate ourselves, make ourselves easy prey, and subject ourselves to his assaults. The end of despair is akin to the end of a hanging rope, and there is nothing more that Satan wants than for you to come to the end of that rope and take your own life, so that he can have you in hell to suffer with him forever. Therefore, our response, and my encouragement to you is the same that Peter gave the Christian believers, **Resist him, firm in your faith, knowing that the same kinds of suffering are being experienced by your brotherhood throughout the world** (1 Peter 5:9). And what is the result? **And after you have suffered a little while, the God of all grace, who has called you to His eternal glory in Christ, will Himself restore, confirm, strengthen, and establish you** (v. 10).

Fifthly, it is okay to lean on both the medicinal and the spiritual remedies that we have access to in this world. God has blessed man with all kinds of knowledge and understanding, and much of this pours into the world via medicine. Some who suffer from depression have chemical imbalances in the brain which require medicine. Others struggle with the burdens of this world and may feel they need medicine when they really on need counseling. I find no problem with those who suffer from depression to seek guidance. I would encourage anyone seeking counseling to do so from a church firmly rooted in Scripture who can point to Christ and the ultimate meaning of life as only being found in Him. While other guidance counselors can assist with navigating through life's ordeals (and I have experienced this myself), they cannot ultimately solve the issue if the answer does not involve the gospel.

Sixthly, take depression one day at a time. Give yourself the ability to heal and recover. If you are a believer, get into the Word and get into a group of other believers who can uphold you. If you are not a believer, I would gently point you to Christ and His Word, but would also nudge you to find groups wherein you can find support to not be completely

---

[3] When Jesus refutes the Pharisees in John 8, He calls them sons of the devil because they were liars and murderers like the devil is. He says, "You are of your father the devil, and your will is to do your father's desires. He was a murderer from the beginning, and does not stand in the truth, because there is no truth in him. When he lies, he speaks out of his own character, for he is a liar and the father of lies" (v. 44).

alone. Many times, it helps us to know that we are not totally alone. There are plenty of stories of soldiers who could keep on fighting in battle simply because their brothers in arms were fighting alongside them.

And lastly, depression is not something that makes you weak. All of us walk different paths of life, and it is usually the best of us who have the deepest struggles, because those struggles are what built up our character to begin with. So if you do suffer from depression, know that you are not defective, not weak, and not worthless because of it, and if you feel you are, I implore you to walk beside me as we continue our journey, one page at a time.

To conclude this chapter, I wanted to share two quotes from Charles Spurgeon, a Baptist preacher who loved Jesus dearly. On one occasion, Spurgeon remarked, "I note that some whom I greatly love and esteem, who are, in my judgment, among the very choicest of God's people, nevertheless, travel most of the way to heaven by night."

This same Spurgeon, on fire for the Lord and full of light, who recognized this malady in others, was also transparent and humble enough to confess, "I know, perhaps as well as anyone, what depression means, and what it is to feel myself sinking lower and lower. Yet at the worst, when I reach the lowest depths, I have an inward peace which no pain or depression can in the least disturb. Trusting in Jesus Christ my Savior, there is a still blessed quietness in the deep caverns of my soul."

Beloved, there is hope. While there is still breath in your lungs and tears left to cry, there is still hope—for you.

3

To Steal Away the Sun

Today is January 19th, 2022. As I write this opening paragraph, recently, I have suffered an immeasurable loss in the death of my dear friend and mentor, Ken Keslar. Ken's passing was sudden and took all of us he knew by surprise. We were not expecting his departure, and the suddenness of his passing made the sting that much more bitter. It was only two days ago.

There is no greater loss in this life that the human experience can relate to than that of death. We may lose a relationship, a job, a home, or a limb, but there is something foreign about death that strikes at the heart—a heaviness at the realization that the one who passes will never be with us in this life again—that people are truly irreplaceable.

What compounds the pain of death is the trail of regrets that follow us in regard to the deceased. Could I have been kinder? Should I have told them that I loved them more often? Could I have spent more time with them instead of making excuses?

For me, my heart broke at my lack of consistency in seeing Ken. We would meet every now and again, grab lunch or breakfast, or briefly text, but it was not the same as when we had first met. Upon Ken taking me under his wing, we met frequently. Once per week or more.

We scoured through the book of Revelation, jumped everywhere in the text of the Old Testament, drew lines back to the New, and had many hours labored over God's Word. These memories with Ken were the bedrock of much spiritual growth, but more important to me was having a relationship with a man who loved the Lord and poured out that love upon me, though I was not worthy of it. Ken was one of the most special men that I have ever met. I miss him dearly to this day and wish I had one more opportunity to tell him that I love him and miss him.

Ken's death left me feeling over-encumbered by grief. I spent much time crying alone not knowing how to deal with the guilt I felt of not giving to Ken the relationship that I feel he deserved to have. To be sure, our time together meant a lot to both of us, but it was the sparing nature of that relationship that ate away at me. I generally do not hold people out at arm's length, but my depression makes it easier to just not do anything or be around anyone—to isolate myself despite the fact that I truly do love people and socialization.

The truth we have to face as mortal creatures is that death is a part of our life experience. Loss is a part of our life because sin is a part of our life, and as Paul writes, **The wages of sin is death** (Rom. 6:23). Because of the fall of Adam and Eve, this world was plunged into sin and darkness. Mankind's very fabric of being was corrupted, but not annihilated. The image of God we were made in, though marred, still remains, yet the reality of death should be enough to give us pause. Something so inescapable has to be dealt with at some point or another because we recognize that death is inevitably coming for us.

As a young child, I used to wonder how God knew when He was going to take me. Was there an invisible counter above my head that only He could see that continued to tick and tock until it hit zero? Was there a date and time stamped into my soul marking the final day I had, down to the very breath? Or was it, perhaps, some spurious decision which was determined by chance? The burning question in my mind was, how does God determine when He's going to take me? I contemplated this question as a young child, I believe, around the age of six, sitting in the bathtub while the water cascaded from the faucet.

In the Bible, David, under the inspiration of the Holy Spirit, pens the following in the book of Psalms: **Your eyes saw my unformed substance; in Your book were written, every one of them, the days that were formed for me, when as yet there was none of them** (139:16). Considering that the fabric of this universe is upheld by the power of the Lord (see Hebrews 1:1–3), we can very easily see how we do not live or exist by our own power. Ken was taken home on a specific day at a specific time which the Lord ordained. One of the frequent struggles for those left behind is the wrestling with the reality that God is control of both life and death. When a loved one passes, we fold our arms, pout our lips, and cry, "God! That's not fair!" After all, God could have kept them here a minute longer, an hour longer, a day, a week, a year. But the inverse is also true. What if God had taken Ken before I had met him? What if God had taken Ken two years after instead? Though my heart weeps at the loss of my best friend in the Lord, it also rejoices that Ken is in the presence of Jesus and that I was able to experience his tutelage and friendship while here on earth.

How we respond to the problem of loss is contingent upon our worldview. The staunch, materialistic atheist sees death as an immovable foe. Despite technological advances, man's life is generally still capped below one-hundred years. Every day, people are still dying in droves. No matter what we do, death marches on to the beat of its own drum. In other words, the atheist in his worldview has nothing but despair when it comes to the issue of loss as it relates to the life of a loved one. If there is no God, then there is no hereafter. No heaven, no hell. Just mere nonexistence—obliteration. Yet, in the Christian worldview, according to the truth of God's word, death is not the end, neither for the believer nor the unbeliever. No, death is a doorway leading us to the hereafter, one to heaven, and one to hell.[4]

When studying the nature of God as it pertains to creation, theologians are careful to make the distinction between man and God by virtue of contrast. God has eternal being. God is. That is, God never

---

[4] In Matthew 7:13, Jesus, speaking of the two gates that lead to the afterlife, says, "Enter by the narrow gate [the gate to eternal life]. For the way is easy that leads to destruction [hell], and those who enter by it are many. For the gate is narrow and the way is hard that leads to life, and those who find it are few."

changes. He's independent and self-existent by His own power. Man, on the other hand, is none of those things. Man is temporal. He does not possess being in the same sense of God because man is in a constant state of decay. Man is becoming. He's born to grow to eventually and inevitably die. This is, again, because of the sin inherent in us and around us. Because of sin, the whole universe groans under its curse. Nothing has been undefiled by sin. Sin is an agent of loss—first, a lost relationship with God, second, a loss of eternal life with Him, and third, a loss of a life free from suffering and pain. All of this to say, loss is an inevitable part of life that we have to deal with. We may delay it or fight against it, but at the end of the day, loss is a problem we as human beings possess.

Now we take time to consider what some painful losses in our lives are. For me, losing Ken was tremendously painful. Mourning is a natural response to the problem of loss: **Rejoice with those who rejoice; mourn with those who mourn** (Rom. 12:15). Suffering loss also has significant impact on us. With Ken gone, life feels different. The day after Ken's passing, I went to the café we frequented and sat at the table where we usually met. I looked out the side window, looked to the doors, hoping to see him walk through with newspaper and Bible in hand. As I got my food, I realized that Ken was not coming through the door again. I would no longer feel his hand on my shoulder as he bellowed, "How are you, young man?" No more life lessons, no more sharing updates in my life. The stark realization that Ken would never see my kids, attend my wedding, or know about any of the major life events that would occur crippled my spirit. I sat at our table listening to R.C. Sproul sermons and reading Scripture. It was the best way I could figure to honor him at that moment. Truly, life will never be the same again without my beloved teacher. But though life for one has ended, the story does not stop. Despite the fact that one day, both Ken and I will be gone, absent from that table in which we use to so frequently meet, God's glory is not halted. His purposes still stand, and it is in light of that truth that we press on toward the final prize. I find it to be no small matter that Ken's final text message to me was Philippians 3:13–14, **Brothers… forgetting what lies behind and straining forward to what**

lies ahead, I press on toward the goal for the prize of the upward call of God in Jesus Christ. I know this is what Ken did until the very end, and it is now what I must do as well.

But why does loss—whether that of life or material possessions so hamstring us in our pursuit of satisfaction? I cannot speak universally to the issue, but I can share some of my thoughts in hopes that these considerations help you garner a new perspective on the matter at hand.

To the first, we live in a material world. We exist in it. There is not a millisecond in which we are not, in some way, interacting with this material world. For most of us, one of the material possessions we own that has high priority is money. It is how we purchase and come to have possessions. Having possessions gives us security in some sense. This is perhaps why debt is so invasive to us—it reminds us that what we have is in some way actually belongs to another. I may receive a paycheck of $1,000, but I may only see $600 after debts are paid for that pay period. Or how about your home? I could not fathom how difficult my life would become if I were to lose my home. To lose my home would most likely mean losing a great majority of things inside of it. Tack on the issue of Arizona's heat and you have a formula for disaster. In my home, I find a great deal of security. I have protection from the elements, increased defenses against intruders, and a place to return to after labor. But just because one has a home does not mean that they are secure. Some of us go to a broken home where our father is missing, and our mother is an alcoholic. Or we come home to a place where the fridge and cabinets are empty, and the electric shut off.

What about the loss of good health? Suffering in the body has an adverse effect on the soul, especially if it is a protracted suffering. It exhausts us and detracts from our quality of life. I can attest to the devastating consequences of my depression and how it continued to shake me every time it reared its ugly head. And when I thought the suffering could not get any worse, I found myself sorely mistaken.

What makes loss so terrible in this life is that as long as we are still breathing, we stand to lose even more. I may curse the heavens because I lost a job opportunity to the next guy, but my bitterness will only extend itself once I lose the next three job opportunities to three other candidates. In other words, we aren't equipped to enjoy losing.

But the issue presses on. We know if only tacitly that we are judged by the outside world based heavily on our possessions. The well-groomed man with a sharp suit will most likely garner more attention and chance in an interview over the man who only has a stained button-up that he last wore in college ten years ago, all other things being equal. The more a person has and the nicer those possessions are, the more lauding is heaped upon him, even if he doesn't truly deserve it. We all want to be friends with those whose possessions and resources are so superabundant that it stands to benefits us as well. And if we have that great abundance? The temptation to be superfluous and fluff our feathers to the world becomes all the more prevalent. After all, in this shallow age of super egoism with its multiple facets of social media flaunting, our desire to boast in ourselves and what we have has never been greater, and if the trend continues the way it has been, will only grow worse. As you can probably see, the problem of loss compounds itself in many instances. For example, consider this linear chain of loss: job, money, partner, home, luxuries, self-worth, comfort, peace, security, and will to live. Though not every circumstance leads to such drastic results, it is easy to see how one loss could potentially influence another if something does not break the successiveness of the chain.

Beyond this, there is another form of loss, though I use the word loss loosely. When I was growing up as a young man, like many young men before me, I began to foster emotional and physical attractions to the opposite sex. Now, I was not the most attractive young man. However, I had an older brother who was made much more fashionably than I. Because of this, I was often overlooked by my female contemporaries. Indeed, there was a higher chance of Jesus making the rocks cry out in worship of Himself than for a female to announce their attraction to me. Day in and day out, I was approached by some female who wanted me to play messenger and relay to my brother a requiem of love. In these moments, I found myself hurt, of low-esteem, and slightly bitter and confused. I felt as though, because of my brother's existence, I had suffered loss—loss of attention, of value, and of dignity. I felt relatively invisible in light of him, and to make matters worse, he was the kind of charitable brother who made sure to emphasize that no one could actually see me. Despite not having lost anything actual, I felt like I had lost something potential, and that hurt me just as much.[5]

If the problem of loss is so pervasive in our life, and as we already established, inevitable, then surely the Scriptures speak to the issue and offers something by way of consolation to mankind in light of it. It is with full assurance that I tell you that not only does the Bible speak about loss, but it also shares with us the struggles of God's people in dealing with it as well.

Perhaps one of the most relevant stories in the Bible surrounding loss is the story of Job, servant of God. Other than Jesus, no one was as intimately familiar with loss as was Job. He was a man with a superabundance of blessings from God that manifested in a boon of material goods. However, upon reading the first chapter of Job, we are told that Job suffers a heavy blow to all of his material possessions. The totality of this loss stretched itself across all that Job possessed, which we read was seven sons and three daughters. **He possessed 7,000 sheep, 3,000 camels, 500 yokes of oxen, and 500 female donkeys, and very many servants, so that this man was the greatest of all the people of the east** (Job 1:3). Estimates of Job's worth in the mere possession of his livestock places him easily beyond 50 million dollars. This does not consider the land, servants, and other resources Job possessed outside of this. In one swift day, Job loses all of his possessions, including his sons and daughters. What happened?

In the first instance of loss, Job learns that the Sabeans fell upon his house and took the oxen and the donkeys and killed a great deal of his servants. After hearing this news, Job receives a second report: that fire from heaven fell and consumed his sheep and the servants with them. Before Job can calibrate, a third report comes in while the second report was still being given! The third report informs Job that the Chaldeans

---

[5] If you struggle with this problem, remember that God in His infinite wisdom knows what to give us and what to keep from us. I am wholly aware that had the Lord given me the desires of my heart, I would have used it to an end leading to death, not to His glory. See Jeremiah 17:9; Proverbs 14:12; Ecclesiastes 9:3.

formed three groups and made a raid on the camels and killed more of Job's servants. And lastly, a fourth report comes to Job that tells him about the death of all of his children via a collapsed house. In the blink of an eye, Job had lost it all. Yet, this was not the end of his suffering. In the words of Cat Power, "Life is hard and gets worse and worse and worse." There is always more to suffer, more to lose, more to despair of. For Job, this saying would only prove itself true.

After suffering the loss of property and his children, Job's response is very indicative of his trust in God: **Then Job arose and tore his robe and shaved his head and fell on the ground and worshiped** (Job 1:20). In ancient, Jewish culture, when one experienced duress or tribulation, they would tear their robes and shave their head or throw dust upon it as a sign of mourning (see Genesis 37:29; Ezra 9:3). And considering the constant succession of reports given unto Job, it is easy to understand why he felt such powerful emotions. However, there is one peculiar statement here about Job's response that may be overlooked. Had Job simply arose, tore his robes, and shaved his head, we could understand this. But what about Job prostrating himself on the floor and worshiping God? Didn't he just, in a moment, lose everything? But Job's worship goes on: **And he said, "Naked I came from my mother's womb, and naked shall I return. The LORD gave, and the LORD has taken away; blessed be the name of the LORD"** (Job 1:21). Job's response to his loss seems strange to our modern ears. When we lose something as simple as our car keys, we enter into disarray. If we misplace our wallet, panic ensues. When we experience the death of a loved one, we are undone.

Now, it is important to point out that when Job suffered tremendous loss, he felt its impact. Job was humbled, in reverence, of his God. He recognized that all he had—the many blessings—were all from Him. Nothing was of Job's own design or power. His God had given unto Job, and in His sovereignty, had allowed what Job possessed to be stripped from him. Job's recognition of this reality did not remove his pain or emotional response. To be sure, we have attachment to our possessions and even more so to our loved ones. To lose them is a bitter thing, and Scripture nowhere forbids our mourning over them in the right contexts. So while Job worshiped God's august sovereignty, he was not leading a procession of celebration throughout his house, nor throwing a banquet feast in honor of this sudden loss. Though I worship God through Ken's death, acknowledge His right as Sovereign over all things, and magnify His goodness for the blessing Ken was to us all, there is a very real sense of pain and trauma that inhabits the reality of Ken's passing, so we as believers have no need to "fake" it. There is no sin in mourning that which has a right to be mourned.

Continuing on through the narrative of Job's loss, we now come into the second chapter where we hear another response to Job's plight. This response comes from none other than Job's wife. After Job loses his children and livestock, Satan strikes him with loathsome sores from the sole of his foot to the crown of his head (Job 2:7). While Job, in his agony, sits amongst the ashes of what remains, he scrapes his sores with broken pottery. Upon seeing this display, Job's wife opens her mouth and says, **"Do you still hold fast your integrity?** *Curse God and die"* (2:9, emphasis mine). Job's wife saw her husband's downtrodden and miserable state. She invoked him to curse God with the expectation that God would strike him dead. This sinful recourse was met by a sharp response. Job replies, **"You speak as one of the foolish women would speak. Shall we receive good from God, and shall we not receive evil?"** (v. 10). The use of foolish from Job did not simply mean a lack of intelligence, though that is certainly implied. Rather, the word was meant as a denouncement toward his wife's impious, wicked response to Job's suffering. It was a moral foolishness—a lack of righteousness and reverence toward God. When Job's wife called him to insult God, she was calling into question God's judgment and sovereign rule. She was lobbing accusations of inadequacy toward God for her husband's state. She was full of misplaced scorn. In other words, her eyes were stuck on the horizontal plane with no recognition or appreciation for the vertical one.

At this juncture, we must now take account of Job's usage of the word *evil*. The apostle James clearly states to us that God cannot be tempted with evil, and He Himself tempts no one (see James 1:13). If this is the case, then it would be prudent of us to understand this word contextually. When Job uses the word evil, he is speaking primarily to that which is bad or unpleasant. There was no moral value assigned to Job's punishment, but there was a level of intolerableness. Job's point was this: if we should receive good from God when we do not deserve it, why should we then turn and complain when God brings calamity to us? Job recognized that unfavorable circumstances are not beyond the scope of God's control. In modern Christianity, we tend to take bad circumstances and say that those are not God's will for us. We must then ask if God did not will it, how did it occur? Is there another, more powerful force in control of evil outside of God? Is there a dualistic relationship between God and Satan?[6] Or is God truly in control of all things, assigning everything its time and purpose? The way in which we answer this question will be detrimental in how we respond to loss— whether our response is that of Job or that of his wife.

So we must now ask, what is it that we have lost, and how will we understand that loss in light of God's revelation? Another pressing question that also influences this question is how we assign value to the things in our lives, whether material or relational. If our value system is askew, then it is likely that our response to loss will also be unbalanced. If we are to view the problem of loss correctly, we must use the Word of God as our scale and trust the balances, no matter which way they fall. Understanding that loss is painful and that we have warrant to mourn it is the first step to lessening the damage that that loss has on our souls. It seems to be that men especially have a hard time expressing external emotions of sorrow, perhaps due to the idea that acts such as crying or mourning is associated with weakness. There is the pervasive idea that men must be stoic and rigid, but this idea is not found in the Scriptures. While men certainly are called to be strong, having faith and courage and resiliency (see 1 Kings 2:1–3; 1 Corinthians 16:13), that does not somehow denote that men cannot express any form of emotion whatsoever. The definitive mark of a man from the Scriptures is the

---

[6] Christian orthodoxy dismisses any notion of a duality between God and Satan. It is not that God and Satan are locked in eternal conflict, fighting for control over the universe. We can observe the sovereignty of God over Satan in the account of Job's suffering. Satan has to request permission from God multiple times to afflict Job, only afflicting him as far as God would allow. Satan can do nothing if he does not have permission from God to do it.

God he vigorously pursues, not his lack of weeping or emotions. A man in the Lord can both weep and lead; they are not mutually exclusive. If this is the case, then we can recognize that like a body healing a physical wound, so too does the soul have a process for healing spiritual and emotional wounds—and that this healing takes time. This is clearly seen in Job's experience, for even after rebuking the impious words of his wife, Job's suffering continues: **Now when Job's three friends heard of all this evil that had come upon him… they made an appointment together to come to show him sympathy and comfort him…. And they sat with him on the ground seven days and seven nights, and no one spoke a word to him, for they saw that his suffering was very great** (see Job 2:11–13).

Job understood his suffering in light of God's sovereignty, but that understanding contextualized the pain and loss—it did not remove it. If I break my leg, the realization of God's sovereignty in that event does not mend the fracture and remove the pain; these events have to play out the way they were intended to play out, pain and all.

When I worked as a manager for a loss prevention department, I had made a fatal mistake in an apprehension, violating all the directives of my company. To stop two thieves from stealing a cart of merchandise, I tackled them through a fire exit, taking them to the ground and wrestling with them. Due to other managers coming and seeing me wrestling with one of the subjects, I decided to disengage him, push him away, and told him to get off the property. He did, and we recovered the merchandise. However, I now had blood on me and all over of my clothes. Fortunately, it was not my own blood, but the copious amounts were an indicator that the subject most likely fell upon something, perhaps a pocketknife or box cutter. I knew at that moment that I was most likely going to get fired. I notified my boss of the event, and for the next week, I had to wait in suspense to find out whether I was going to lose my job. For that entire week, I was petrified. Many of the days, I was on the floor of my apartment crying bitterly that I had committed such an erroneous action. To make matters worse, I had just started this job less than two months prior after being promoted to it. I was stuck in a lease three hours away from what I called home and knew if I lost this job, I'd have to regress to something that paid significantly less. I felt that all I had worked so hard for was going to slip through my fingers.

I prayed about the situation repeatedly. Despite knowing that God was in control, the anxiety and pain remained. To be sure, the impact of potential or even actual loss can be significantly reduced by clinging to the Word of God in faith. For me, this is where the rubber met the road. I had the intellectual knowledge of God's sovereignty, but did I have the faith to make that knowledge come alive in my own life? After all, the demons knew who Jesus was, yet that knowledge only served to further condemn them in their rebellion. At this time, I did not have the right view on the situation, so the pressures surrounding me often overwhelmed me. I let the circumstance of my life affect my faith when it should have been the other way around. In situations that overwhelm us, we would do well to remember the cry of the father whose son had an unclean spirit: **"I believe; help my unbelief!"** (see Mark 9:24).

So what is it that you have lost? Have you taken the proper time to mourn and process it? Do you take your pain to the Lord in prayer knowing that He cares about you? Have you gone to His Word for comfort? As James says, God draws near to those who draw near to Him (see James 4:8).

Before Ken's passing, I would read stories of faith involving believers who suffered tumultuous losses. The amount of faith these individuals had in God and their perspective on their loss was akin to that of Job's. This often left me confused. I'd think to myself, "How in the world can you lose your wife and have such composure? You just lost your entire family in a natural disaster. How can you lean on the Lord? How has your sorrow not torn you to pieces?" However, after Ken's passing, through tears and pain, God began to show me through His Word and through His Spirit how it is possible to suffer loss and cling to Him in ways not yet done before, and perhaps a word of clarification here may be helpful. When I speak of this comfort of God, or leaning on God, I do not mean simply treating God like a crutch by using Him as a Band-Aid on a gaping wound. Often times, people will view evil or suffering as a negative force outside the scope of God's sovereignty and then use God as a positive force in spite of it, but I am not speaking of facades here. I am speaking of the reality of having fellowship with the Lord, which when faced with loss that is beyond your control and understanding, drives you to Him in dependence and gratitude for His comforts.

Through the loss of Ken, I have a deeper appreciation for my Lord, life, and the relationships with those around me. I spend more time in the Word and in prayer. I rely on the grace of God more. Because God is sovereign, He can use even the greatest losses we experience for our good. In fact, this is one of the promises of God that Paul shares with us in Romans 8:28: **And we know that for those who love God all things work together for good, for those who are called according to His purpose.** What falls outside of this scope? Nothing. And in fact, probably more times than we know, the losses in our life are probably good things. Why do I say this?

The human heart, ever since the fall, has been an idol factory—and a productive one at that. Jeremiah writes in Jeremiah 17:9, **The heart is deceitful above all things, and desperately wicked; who can know it?** Elsewhere, speaking of the heart, Jesus says, **"Don't you see that whatever enters the mouth goes into the stomach and then out of the body? But the things that come out of the mouth come from the heart, and these make a man unclean. For out of the heart comes evil thoughts, murder, adultery, sexual immorality, theft, false testimony, slander"** (Matthew 15:17–19). Because of this, we often place things of this world above God, and the list of idols we have is non-exhaustive. So in one sense, our loss could very well be God doing us a favor, even if at the moment we do not recognize it.

To understand this, we do not have to look very far. In his epistle to the Philippians, Paul writes the following about loss he suffered in his life: **But whatever gain I had, I counted as loss for the sake of Christ. Indeed, I count everything as loss because of the surpassing worth of knowing Christ Jesus my Lord. For His sake I have suffered the loss of all things and count them as rubbish, in order that I may gain Christ** (Philippians 3:7–8). Paul, before his conversion, had everything a man of the Jews could want. He had power, reputation, resources, authority, and knowledge. He was esteemed by the highest

Jewish religious leaders, a man whose devotion to the law of God was unblemished. Yet, despite these many accolades, Paul realized that losing them in light of his eternity was not loss, but gain. After all, what worth are those things here on earth which remain once we depart? My stocks remain, my possessions remain, and my loved ones remain. I can take nothing with me because I do not hold the keys over death. That special authority is reserved for Christ alone (see Revelation 1:18). What possesses ultimate value in the final analysis is not what I have stake in on this earth, but the very soul within me—the one that will one day face God who is a consuming fire (Hebrews 12:29). Perhaps no clearer statement about the distinction of loss has been made than that which comes from our Lord's mouth. In Matthew 16:26, Jesus asks the very pointed question: **"For what will it profit a man if he gains the whole world and forfeits his soul? Or what shall a man give in return for his soul?"** The point Jesus is here making is that the soul is priceless. There is nothing in creation for a man worth more to him (second to God) than that of his own soul. It is in this light that Paul denounces his former possessions as *skybalon*, which is the Greek word rightfully translated as "animal excrement." It is not that Paul's possessions were inherently evil, but rather, they became worthless in comparison to the glory of Christ's riches and salvation. Paul recognized that what he formerly possessed served as a barrier to him in having a right relationship with God, and realizing that these titles and possessions had to be discarded for the sake of following Jesus, Paul regarded them as worthless in light of having Christ. If we, like Paul, have our soul right, then we do not need to worry about the loss of things here on earth, because we know they were never meant to be with us forever.[7] However, having the right perspective on those things in which we will inevitably lose will only help us further rejoice in them. Outside of our idols, if we understand our possessions to be gifts from our Lord to be enjoyed while we have them, and live with thankful hearts, then we maximize those things and can live in gratitude of them in light of their

---

[7] Solomon writes in Ecclesiastes 5:15, "Everyone comes naked from their mother's womb, and as everyone comes, so they depart. They take nothing from their toil that they can carry in their hands."

disappearing. Again, this does not mean the loss of those things will not cause pain, but we know we will not have to suffer it alone because God is with us.

One of Jesus's teachings about this subject stands out to me. It is found in Matthew 6:19–21 where we read the following words of Christ: **"Do not store up for yourselves treasures on earth, where moth and vermin destroy, and where thieves break in and steal. But store up for yourselves treasures in heaven, where moths and vermin do not destroy, and where thieves do not break in and steal. For where your treasure is, there your heart will be also."** Could this teaching be any clearer? If while on earth we invest in material things over the salvation of our souls, what good is it, especially in light of the fact that we're only here for a brief while? Though we may have confidence in tomorrow, it is never promised. In another parable regarding possessions (Yes, Jesus taught quite a few!), Jesus says, **"The land of a rich man produced plentifully, and he thought to himself, 'What shall I do, for I have nowhere to store my crops?' And he said, 'I will do this: I will tear down my barns and build larger ones, and there I will store all my grain and my goods. And I will say to my soul, "Soul, you have ample goods laid up for many years; relax, eat, drink, and be merry."' But God said to him, 'Fool! This night your soul is required of you, and the things you have prepared, whose will they be?' So is the one who lays up treasure for himself and is not rich toward God"** (Luke 12:16–21).

At this juncture, one may turn around and ask, "Hey, what's the big deal? Jesus is always talking about loss, but He's the Son of God. He came in the full power of God, expelling demons, feeding thousands, turning water into wine, and raising the dead. What could He possibly know about my loss?" Thankfully for us, the Scriptures have always revealed God as a person of compassion and intimate understanding regarding man's plight, and in fact, this revelation is nowhere more visceral than in the incarnation of Christ. Generally speaking, we tend to view loss as that which was taken from us, but there is another side to that coin—that which is given up.

In the incarnation of Christ, we must first consider what Christ had before He condescended into human flesh. In the beginning of John's gospel, John writes of Jesus: **In the beginning was the Word, and the Word was with God, and the Word was God. He was in the beginning with God. All things were made through Him, and without Him was not anything made that was made** (John 1:1–3). In this short opening, we are bombarded with rich and deep theological truths. First, we see a description of Christ's eternality. "In the beginning" is the English translation for the Greek *en arche*, which otherwise could be stated as, "As far back as you wish to go." No matter how far back one goes on the timeline, the Word is there. There is no point in time that the Word was not. Jesus precedes time as we know it.

Next, John writes that the Word was with God. Here, the Word and God are distinguished, yet in the very next clause, we are told that the Word was God. How can this be? First, when we read that the Word was with God, we turn our attention to the Greek. Because the New Testament was written in Greek, the deepest sense of a meaning we can derive from the Bible is from its original language and context. In the Greek, the word "with" is *pros*, which means to be facing in a direction. In another way of putting it, we can say that the Word was face to face with God. This phrase speaks to the two persons being distinct and within proximity of one another personally, indicating that the Word and God have a relationship. Yet, we now look to that third clause—the Word was God.

Because we allow the context of Scripture to define itself, when we read these words about the Word being God, we understand John as writing to the being or substance of the Word. In many passages in the Bible, God the Father is simply referred to as God. In fact, this is how the apostle Paul usually refers to God. So John can refer to both the person of God and to the being of God in the same sentence because he rightly understood this distinction. The Word has the same nature as God and is a distinct person from God the Father.

To drive his point home about the Word being God, John emphasizes that the Word was with God in the beginning. If we try to make the argument that the Word was created, John removes this opportunity, for the Word was with God in the beginning. Now, one may attempt to assert here that the "beginning" John is referring to is the beginning of creation. However, in the next sentence, John clearly creates two separate and exclusive categories: the created and the eternal. John writes that the entirety of all things created was made through the Word. If the Word was created, He would be a part of the created category, thus He would have had to create Himself before He was in existence! Because we know this is impossible, we can safely remove that option and rightly understand John as establishing the divinity of the Word, who would come down into the world in the person of Christ.

Before Jesus was incarnated, He shared an intimate, eternal relationship with the Father in heaven in glory. To come down into this world and represent mankind, the Word had to give up, or lay aside, His divine prerogative. Paul writes of this truth in his epistle to the Philippians: **Have this mind among yourselves, which is yours in Christ Jesus, who, though He was in the form of God, did not count equality with God a thing to be grasped, but emptied Himself, by taking the form of a servant, being born in the likeness of men** (Philippians 2:5–7).

For Christ to represent us, He had to become like us in our humanity. The Lord of glory, the King of kings, is born in a dirty, run-down manger in Bethlehem amongst the mud and soil of the animals, clad in grime.[8] Christ gives up His authority, His riches in heaven, His glory, to meet mankind where we are, so that when He had come as a man, **He humbled Himself by becoming obedient to the point of death— even to death on a cross** (vv. 7c–8). Throughout His earthly ministry, Christ did not enjoy the luxuries of the ancient world. He did not often have money, was persecuted for His teachings by the religious leaders of the day and suffered many injustices. Regarding His poverty, Jesus says, **"Foxes have holes, and birds of the air have nests, but the Son of Man has nowhere to lay His head"** (Luke 9:58). In fact, when Jesus and His disciples pay a temple tax, Jesus instructs Peter to go fishing and to take the shekel from the mouth of the first fish that comes up (see Matthew 17:24–27). From having everything to having nowhere to lay your head is quite the transition—and quite the loss. But the

---

[8] See Luke 2:7, 8–12, 16.

material comforts that Christ lost were a mere shadow of that which He would lose to fulfill His mission of saving sinners. In the crucifixion of Christ, Jesus would not only lose His life,[9] but He would lose the most valuable thing a person can possess—a right relationship with God. On the cross, Christ became accursed.[10] He took on the full penalty of sin, bore the full weight of God's eternal wrath, and was forsaken by God[11]—severed from Him and relinquished to the darkest depths of suffering—and drank down the dregs of that wrathful cup which God had given unto Him to drink.[12] There was not a single drop left of God's wrath for the sin that Jesus atoned for.[13] The God of the universe with all authority, all power, all majesty, and all glory, came down in the form of a servant to die for sinners.

These are only a few, but vital ways, in which Jesus suffered loss. But what Jesus lost, He gave up voluntarily. He sacrificed. And He did so for rebellious sinners who hated Him, rejected Him, mocked Him, and put Him on the cross. Yet, despite His loss, because of His obedience, God has highly exalted Christ, rewarded Him, and now Christ sits at the right hand of God in eternal glory.

Though we may suffer loss on this earth, we stand to gain something far beyond this world when we place our faith in Christ and repent of our sins. And once this life is over, it is then that we enter into glory with God, Christ, and the Holy Spirit, worrying about loss no more.

But perhaps the most fundamental question we can ask at this juncture is this: do we trust in God? Do we trust in the wisdom of God and the purposes of God—why He takes today what He could have taken tomorrow? Do we trust in His Word that He works all things for good? Do we esteem the blood of Christ and the salvation it purchased as our highest treasure or cling desperately to what we have here on earth? Do we, like Paul, trust that what God gives us in Jesus is greater than it all? The closer we come to terms with the answers to these questions, the better we will be able to handle the problem of

---

[9] See Matthew 27:27–56.

[10] See Galatians 3:13, cf. Deuteronomy 21:22–23.

[11] See Matthew 27:46.

[12] See Matthew 26:42.

[13] See Hebrews 10:10–14.

loss. And although loss is painful, it does not have to mark the end. We can, because of Christ, view loss as inconsequential in comparison to what it is we have to gain. With Paul, we can declare, **I consider that our present sufferings are not worth comparing with the glory that will be revealed in us** (Romans 8:18) because by the power of God, there is one thing that cannot be lost once obtained—eternal life in Christ. Though our bodies may fade and our possessions crumble, we hold fast to this one truth, that God in Christ by the power of His Spirit has atoned for our sins, reconciled us to God, and has given us an imperishable inheritance through Jesus. In this life we may suffer loss, but we will never be lost again.

4

Before the Pouring Began

Allll of us, at some point or another, have been impacted by some form of trauma. Trauma is not a one-size fits all type of ordeal, but rather, varies from person to person and is influenced by many factors. I may find an experience rather harrowing whereas another person in the same situation may simply shrug their shoulders and give an "it is what it is" response. What may linger in my mind and heart for years may only be an afterthought in the mind of another. For each one of us, we have to define our trauma as it relates to us. This is not to say that there is not a general or universe standard or guideline in which is not useful in figuring out whether something is traumatic, but it is to say that we need to take our approach to trauma on a case-by-case basis.

Before we endeavor to speak of trauma or traumatic experiences, I want to give a brief definition that will provide the framework for this chapter. Trauma is a result of some event or circumstance (whether singular or protracted) that detrimentally affects a person whether physically, mentally, emotionally, or psychologically—oftentimes affecting all four. To demonstrate how this plays out, I'll provide a brief example below.

Every Saturday morning, a group of my friends gather online to play a game called Dungeons & Dragons. In this game, each player creates a character. This character is assigned a race, such as human, elf, or dwarf, and an accompanying class or job, such as a knight, archer, or thief. However, there is one player who creates and controls the world in which the other players operate. This person is referred to as the game master. One of the elements that all game masters generally ask their players for is their character's backstory—who they are, where they came from, what their goal is, and if there are any motivating factors driving them. The game master then weaves the multi-faceted elements of each character and brings them together in a "party" in which they operate and explore the world.

In one campaign with my friends, I am the game master. One of my players created a character named Mac, who is a pirate who had an uncanny fear of the ocean and seafaring and was repulsed at the idea of leading the team in any given scenario. The other players had to take time to figure out why Mac was so afraid of the things that generally attract pirates to begin with. They soon came to find out that Mac was adopted into the pirate family of a famous captain. One day while out on the high seas, Mac took the initiative to help sail the boat, but had made a fatal error. This error caused the boat to sink and for the entire crew to perish, save Mac. Because of this, Mac became terrified of the ocean, sailing, and leading. With one simple mistake, Mac lost his father figure and all of his friends who had gone through significant effort to adopt him into their family.

In other words, Mac experienced an event so severe that it had dramatic repercussions on his psyche, his worldview, and his behaviors. He experienced trauma.

Some other symptoms that manifested in Mac's trauma were reoccurring nightmares of the incident and inability to obtain meaningful rest. This event that transpired in time's past was so impactful that it destroyed Mac's ability to function in the future when he was needed, leading to even more casualties out on the seas. The internal consequences Mac suffered externally affected those around Mac. It became an unintentionally corroding agent to those who associated with him.

I labor to say this for the sake of illustrating the long arm of trauma's reach and how it can be an easy catalyst for a journey into depression, or a medium in which depression continues to exist, which Mac often manifested in his journeys.

But how can we know for certain that trauma has meaningfully impacted us? Well, each individual person will have to wrestle honestly with themselves about it. If there has been an experience in your life that has left a mark on you in a way that other experiences have not, and this to your detriment, then it is more than likely you are dealing with trauma. The kind of experience that you find traumatic is also not wholly relevant in the sense that trauma can take place in a myriad of different ways. For example, one may have a fear of highways due to getting into a near fatal car accident, whereas another person, such as my wife, fears abandonment which stems back to a traumatic nightmare she had in her childhood of being left alone in a forest by her father. Now, her nightmare was not drawing from any real event. Her father had never led her into the forest only to let go of her hand and say, "Good luck," as he walks away. Yet even though this was clearly an event that was immaterial, the impact of the event was significant enough to set a foundation for a fear that would soon begin to permeate in her life.

In other instances, your trauma may occur without your realizing it. Years ago, I was previously married. My marriage fell apart, and I eventually moved across the country to be closer to family and away from the wreckage of a bad relationship. For a while, I felt like I was okay. There had not seemed to have been any residual effects in my life by the past relationship. I was, at times, in contact with women in my new area, and though none of those relationships developed into anything long-term or sustaining, I still was able to make some small connections with other people.

That was until I met my wife. At first, there were no issues. But after the relationship began gaining some traction, I began to have guilt feelings about my past relationship. I had felt guilty because I knew in the past that I had had sexual relations and that if I could remember those, that somehow, I was being mentally unfaithful. I began to do this with everything that could even remotely have some kind of overlay to my past. The guilt and anxiety became so bad for me that at times, I thought my wife would have been better off with someone else. Day in and day out was a nightmare. I would talk to my wife about it, and she would always reassure me that there was nothing wrong with me and that I was overthinking things. She was right, but at the moment, I felt like my world was collapsing.

As time passed, I soon realized that I had a lot of damage dealt to me in the past that I had overlooked for the simple fact that nothing prompted me to face it. When I entered into a new relationship and it got serious, then I began having struggles about being in that new relationship, perhaps because I had felt like I was not permitted to have another one due to my failures. To be sure, my past relationship was full of trauma. I had mistakenly believed that because I had jumped out of the fire, I was no longer burning. But as I learned the hard way, you don't need to be in the fire for the fire to be on you. I may have fled the environment in which my trauma thrived; however, I never came to grips with the fact that I was still burning and that once I put out the flames consuming me, that I still needed to tend to my wounds. Those who have escaped domestic abuse relationships can most likely relate to this concept.

It may be that you have traumas you are not wholly aware of. That is okay. If you do have trauma that manifests itself, then you will be better equipped to deal with it when it arises, and this also includes impending trauma that all of will have to inevitably face in our lives.

The task I will endeavor to undertake in this chapter will be twofold. Because there are multiple traumas, I believe that covering them all would be beyond the scope of this work. However, I do wish to write about a few different forms of trauma that I find to be more prevalent, especially in our day and age.

Throughout this chapter, I will be making appeals to incidents of trauma drawn from biblical narratives. Because of this, it is important for us to engage the biblical texts existentially. When we read the Bible, we have a general tendency to be so detached from the text that we sometimes forget that much of biblical literature is historical narrative involving real individuals and experiences. We read the harrowing account of Abraham having to take his only son of promise, Isaac, up to the mount Moriah to be sacrificed on the altar, only to be stopped by God when the knife is raised. Can you imagine the suspense? The agony? The raw, unmitigated emotion that Abraham was experiencing climbing that mountain with the son he had waited so long to have?

When we place ourselves into the shoes and perspective of the characters we read about, that is reading the Scriptures existentially. R.C. Sproul, in his book, *Knowing the Scriptures*, quotes Martin Luther on this point. Luther says, *"When you open the book containing the gospels and read or hear how Christ comes here or there, or how someone is brought to Him, you should therein perceive the sermon or the gospel through which He is coming to you, or you are being brought to Him. For the preaching of the gospel is nothing else than Christ coming to us, or we being brought to Him."*

The few topics that I will aim to address as it relates to trauma is abandonment, abortion, guilt, sin, and abuse. Because the problem of loss, including death, was considered in the last chapter, I will not readdress it here again. With that being said, if there are topics of trauma outside the scope of this work, I believe that the foundational principles herein can still apply, but that does not prohibit you from going beyond this work to find additional resources to aid you in your battle against trauma.

ABANDONMENT

The trauma of abandonment is far spread. All of us, to some degree, have felt abandoned. Some of us experience the fallout of that abandonment with much more severity than others. Some of us have been abandoned by parents, or friends, or spouses. Even worse is that there are many individuals today who believe that they have even been abandoned by God.

But what constitutes abandonment? For now, we can say that abandonment is the leaving or disappearance of a person literally or in principle. I say in principle because some forms of abandonment are not physical. A spouse, for example, has abandoned their partner when they decide to commit adultery and disavow their marriage covenant.

They have abandoned their spouse in the deepest possible means. Some spouses decide that they have "fallen out of love" and decide to turn off all forms or modes of affection, care, and compassion for their spouses. They are still physically present, but they have abandoned their duties as a marriage partner, and by virtue of that, have abandoned their partners. Some experience abandonment that takes place in their dreams, and others experience abandonment on a frequent basis, such as having friends and family cancel plans on them lackadaisically. Or perhaps the abandonment takes place of a parent who, despite knowing better, refused to take care of their health, resulting in a premature death, and by abandoning their health, they ended up abandoning their family. Then there could be the friend or family member who shared the same beliefs as you for a time, but then abandoned those beliefs, thus, in some sense, you feel as though they abandoned you too.

But why does abandonment hurt so badly? I believe that there are many reasons, but perhaps no more pressing than the reason that being abandoned by another is something that we recognize as a declaration of our worth, even if subconsciously. If my spouse commits adultery and abandons me for another, it would be easy to let my thoughts spiral out of control and feel as though the reason why my spouse abandoned me was because I was not good enough in her eyes, and that she had found someone better than me, thus reducing my worth. If my spouse could come to think so lowly of me as to break our lifelong vows, including "for better or for worse," then how could I ever trust anyone in my life not to abandon me like she did when there was the highest expectation of her that she wouldn't?

Another common experience is a parent who abandons their child. The child will feel the repercussions. The first thought will most likely be, "My father/mother did not want me. I wasn't good enough for them. They didn't love me." It is a hard battle to fight against the abandonment of flesh of blood. To be renounced by your parent/s in such a way is devastating, namely because God's design was for the family to be an intact unit built upon His truth and His law, which heavily emphasizes the family priority.

What makes matters worse is that both parents are essential to the makeup of their children. We read in Proverbs 1:8–9 for example, **Hear, my son, your father's instruction, and forsake not your mother's teaching, for they are a graceful garland for your head and pendants for your neck.** Proverbs 2:1–5 follows the same formula: **My son, if you receive my words and treasure up my commandments with you, making your ear attentive to wisdom and inclining your heart to understanding, yes, if you call out for insight and raise your voice for understanding, if you seek it like silver and search for it as for hidden treasures, then you will understand the fear of the LORD and find the knowledge of God**, and again in Proverbs 3:1–2, **My son, do not forget my teaching, but let your heart keep my commandments, for length of days and years of life and peace they will add to you.**

Being abandoned by one's mother or father is painful because with the abandonment of a parent comes the loss of guidance and instruction. It cripples one's esteem and puts pressure on them to grow up much faster than they would have had to, had one or both parents been present.

In an attempt to comfort the child, one may tell them, "Your parent/s loved you, but they weren't ready to be a parent yet." This is a heinous excuse. What it is communicating is that the father (or mother) was ready to perform the act of procreation, with the chance of procreating, but were not willing to do the hard work that comes with raising a child. It is in essence telling the child, "I had to choose between an easy life without you or a harder life with you, and you didn't make the difference." That kind of life lesson will be agonizing in light of having to experience other children enjoying their relationship with their own parents.

Abandonment also hurts deeply because it is not something we anticipate or expect. When I meet people, I do not say, "I would like to be your friend, but only if there is a high chance that you will, either soon or in the near future, abandon me." To the contrary, when I meet people, I want to know that they are trustworthy and dependable. I want to feel like if worse comes to worst, that they will be there for me. We want people in our lives who are resiliently faithful. We want the type of close friends who emulate the saying, "When the going gets tough, the tough get going." If we knew that the people in our lives would eventually abandon us, we most likely would not attempt to build any meaningful bond with them.

Abandonment is also something out of our control. We hate that as human beings, don't we? In a perfect world, we'd have control over all components of our life because man's innate desire as a sinner is to be autonomous apart from God. We want to be self-rulers and live according to the way we see fit, which means we inevitably want control over everything that touches on our life experiences, but we have no power over whether someone chooses to stay or leave. We can influence that decision to be sure, but we can't control it. Even if we do everything right, there's still a chance that we could be betrayed or abandoned by someone that we love.

Perhaps what makes abandonment worse is that once experienced, it destroys any meaningful sense of security in our lives, gives rise to anxiety, and makes the world feel uncertain. After a while, we come to expect being abandoned and then act in that light, unintentionally becoming a self-fulfilling prophecy. We become so terrified of abandonment that we subconsciously push people away from us so that they can't abandon us to begin with, and then turn around and claim that they abandoned us anyway! If you are telling yourself, "Wow, that does seem pretty illogical," you would be right. That is because abandonment plants seeds of doubt and fear into the depths of our heart, and once those seeds spring roots, they are terribly difficult to kill, and as the roots of abandonment spread, they begin to influence our behavior because they affect the way our mind operates. Our thoughts become tainted, and we begin to interpret everybody's actions through the lens that they're going to hurt us at some point or another.

More than once in my relationship with my wife, there have been moments of conflict simply because my wife felt like I was abandoning her. The "abandonment" she was experiencing was not truly abandonment by definition, but according to her fear, it was bona fide abandonment to the superlative degree. That is because people who struggle with abandonment issues seem to operate off of potentialities instead of actualities because potentialities and fear are easily married.

You see, more often than not, we fear what may be and not what is. I am sure in my wife's mind, she can perceive of the potential situation where I open the front door, walk through, close it, and never return. Her fears—while based on the potential—are inadvertently actualized when she allows her emotions to guide her instead of her mind. This has manifested itself before in our marriage. There have been times when I have made plans with another, only for her to feel as though I had excluded her or had chosen to do something with that person at that time over doing something with her. In her response to me, she operates on the assumption of that fear's accuracy and not the actual situation at hand.

In another way of putting it, my wife's fears cause her to develop self-defense mechanisms. Some of these come by instinct. It is akin to a dog who has suffered physical abuse by the only human owner they have known. The dog is rescued, put in a cage, and taken to a shelter. Whenever another human draws near, the dog recedes as far back as the cage allows, growls, hisses, and whimpers, and may even bite—despite the fact that the new human interacting with them intends them no harm. That is because abandonment issues create trust issues. Recall that abandonment leads to insecurity. Insecurity denotes a lack of trust, either in one's own ability, in others around them, the environment, or the situation. These makes fighting the battle that much more difficult.

Imagine for a moment that you are a soldier in war. The battle you're engaged in is at a stalemate. Any small factor can change the outcome of the fight. As you toil in combat with your allies, they decide that it's best they don't risk their necks. They tuck tail and run the other way, leaving you severely disadvantaged. Then, you receive a message that the reinforcements and supplies that are supposed to come may or may not come through for you. You're outnumbered and left to die by your allies, you have no idea if the supplies and support you need is even going to show up, and the enemy is pressing in on you. How are you feeling?

Let's change the scenario slightly. All factors are the same except in this case, your allies tell you that no matter what may come, they will continue fighting beside you. And as you fight, over the hills beyond, you see the reinforcements rushing to your aid. With your allies beside you and hope coming over the horizon, wouldn't you feel that much more motivated to survive knowing that victory was imminent if you could just hang in there for a little longer? Wouldn't faithful friends and comrades motivate you to press on despite being in a war-torn trench?

Knowing that our loved ones are there for us in our corner and are not going anywhere is a strong bolster to our spirit. However, the opposite edge of this sword is equally sharp. If we are the boxer without a coach in our corner to give us guidance or encouragement in between rounds, we're at a disadvantage against our opponent who has their coach pumping them up. Life is difficult enough with friends surrounding us. How much more so when those friends leave us to fight alone?

If anyone in the Bible was familiar with abandonment, it was Jesus. Recall that Christ came to the earth as the Messiah of the world. He performed innumerable miracles that authenticated His ministry and His claims of being God in the flesh, yet despite these revelatory actions and words, Jesus was rejected time and time again. In fact, John writes in the opening chapter of his gospel, **[Jesus] was in the world, and the world was made through Him, yet the world did not know Him. He came to His own, and His own people did not receive Him** (John 1:10–11). The lack of the peoples' knowledge as it pertained to the person of Christ was not due to the insufficiency of Christ's revelation to the people, but rather due to their abandonment of the truth of God which was a direct abandonment of the Christ who came as the Way, the truth, and the life (see John 14:6). Jesus's "own people" were the Jews, for Jesus was born from Jewish descent. The people of Israel were obligated to fidelity as it pertained to God's Word. They should have recognized Jesus as the Messiah prophesied by the Old Testament, yet in their hardness of heart, they repudiated Jesus to their own demise.

This is not to say that Jesus was a loner His entire ministry. Jesus had His core twelve disciples. He had large crowds of followers at different times, hanging onto His every word—until that word became too difficult. Then they abandoned Jesus.[14] He wasn't worth it. Yet, at

---

[14] See John 6:60–71.

the moment it mattered most, Jesus suffered the abandonment of His closest friends, His chosen twelve disciples, in the hour of need.[15]

Yet even this abandonment was not the worst that Jesus suffered. On the cross, Jesus became the sin bearer, taking on the penalty of sin and its curse upon Himself, in the place of those who would repent and believe to make reconciliation to God an actuality by tearing down the wall that separates man and God—sin.

Because God is holy, He cannot overlook our sin. Because God is just, He must punish it. The only way that sinners can escape this just judgment is by trusting in Christ as Lord and Savior and repenting of their sins, turning to God for forgiveness and mercy. In this, a sinner is reconciled to God because on the cross, Christ paid for their sins by taking them upon Himself and paying off the debt in full. In exchange, Christ gives the sinner His perfect righteousness. Why is this so important?

For Christ to save you, He had to take your place on the cross, where you deserve to be. He had to experience the full penalty of sin. Part of this penalty is being completely abandoned by God, left to die utterly alone. We read the sorrowful cry of Christ, **"Eli, Eli, lama sabachthani?" that is to say, "My God, My God, why have You forsaken Me?"** (see Matthew 27:46).

On the cross, God turned His back on Christ, abandoned Him fully to the wrath and justice that sinners deserve. Christ did not have the comfort of God, the relationship to God, or the help of God. I cannot imagine any form of abandonment to be an iota as severe as the abandonment that Jesus suffered from the Father. It was this knowledge of what was to come that causes Jesus to sweat drops like blood in the garden before His crucifixion. Jesus suffered abandonment that you and I could never fathom this side of heaven. But the same kind of abandonment that Christ suffered on earth to pay off the debt of His people's sins is the same abandonment that sinners in hell will

---

[15] See Mark 14:50. While Peter followed Jesus to the courtyard, his abandoning Jesus was the worst betrayal of all. When asked of his association with Jesus, Peter emphatically denied knowing Jesus three times to save himself. At the cross, however, it appears that many stood by to witness Jesus's crucifixion (see Matthew 27:55–56; Mark 15:40; Luke 23:49; John 19:25).

experience for an eternity. It will be an insufferable anguish that will never be quenched, nor lessened in severity. **It is a fearful thing to fall into the hands of the living God** (Hebrews 10:31), **for our God is a consuming fire** (12:29). This solemn warning from Scripture is given as a mercy to drive us toward the cross of Christ where forgiveness and hope can be found.

When I view the problem of abandonment, what I observe is that more often than not, abandonment is derived from the frailty of the human will. God did not make man to forsake fellow man, nor did He create the universe in chaos. The brokenness that leads to our forsaking others or ourselves is, as we said, a result of our sin. The fidelity that man should operate according to is lost in his corruption. Christ's atoning sacrifice restores what was severely damaged by the Fall between mankind, but it only could come by way of Christ being abandoned Himself.

What makes Jesus's being abandoned by God is that He did not deserve it. Christ never sinned, nor rebelled against God. What makes that account so astonishing is that in mercy and love, Christ took our sins upon Himself for us. He was abandoned by God so that we wouldn't be. As Charles Spurgeon once said, *"You stand before God as if you were Christ because Christ stood before God as if He were you."*[16] On the other hand, if anyone deserves to be utterly forsaken by God, it is us. We are the most faithless, rebellious creatures of God's creation.

But why is God so faithful? It has to do with His character. When we look through the Scriptures, we are constantly reminded of God's faithfulness. One of the ways that God displays this for us is by way of covenant. A covenant is similar to a contract. In a contract, two parties agree upon certain conditions, add consequences for breaking it, and allow for permissions to terminate the binding of the contract should one party violate the agreements listed therein. The idea of a contract generally assumes the shared authority between both persons entering into the contract. However, God does not make contracts with man, as if man were on equal footing with God. A covenant, for simplicity's sake, is an oath bound relationship between two or more parties. There

---

[16] See 2nd Corinthians 5:21 and Galatians 3:13.

are different kinds of covenants in the Bible that God enacts and enters into with His chosen people, but they all have one common thread: God is the author, initiator, and finisher of His covenant.

What makes God's covenant so radically different from all other ideas of covenant is that in the schema of the divine covenant in view, God swears by Himself to fulfill it. He writes the conditions of the covenant and ensures that the covenant is fulfilled. And why does God choose certain persons to enter into a covenant with? Is it because they are worthy of it? Perhaps they are a people more in number, or more righteous, and therefore more likely to reap higher rewards for God. Perhaps their merits before God impressed Him enough for God to enter a covenant with them. Or perhaps God just rolled the proverbial dice.

No.

The reason why God chooses who He chooses cannot be fully understood by us here on earth, but the Scriptures do give us a pattern to see who God chooses and why. For example, in Deuteronomy 7:6–8, God says, **"For you [Israel] are a people holy to the LORD your God. The LORD your God has chosen you to be a people for His treasured possession, out of all the peoples who are on the face of the earth. It was not because you were more in number than any other people that the LORD set his love on you and chose you, for you were the fewest of all peoples, but it is because the LORD loves you and is keeping the oath that He swore to your fathers, that the LORD has brought you out with a mighty hand and redeemed you from the house of slavery, from the hand of Pharaoh king of Egypt."**

God makes it clear that His choosing and covenanting with Israel had nothing to do with Israel. God had ransomed Israel from the bondage of Egypt, made them His own people, and then entered into covenant with them as their Sovereign. Israel contributed nothing to earn or merit this covenant. This sentiment is echoed by Paul in the New Testament: **For consider your calling, brothers: not many of you were wise according to worldly standards, not many were powerful, not many were of noble birth. But God chose what is foolish in the world to shame the wise; God chose what is weak in the world to shame the strong; God chose what is low and despised in the world,**

even things that are not, to bring to nothing things that are, so that no human being might boast in the presence of God (1 Corinthians 1:26–29).

A clear example of God making a covenant that is based solely upon Himself can be found in Genesis 15 with the story of Abraham. In this account, God promises Abraham an heir who would come from his own loins. This may seem like a minor detail, but up until this point, Abraham's wife, Sarah, was barren, and both her and Abraham were of old age, beyond the years of bearing children. Abraham wanted desperately to have a son to call his own, so God, in grace, promised Abraham that He would give him a son. However, God promised much more: **[God] took [Abraham] outside and said, "Look at the sky and count the stars, if you are able to count them." Then [God] said to [Abraham], "So shall your offspring be"** (see Genesis 15:5). So here, we have a promise of God. But God also promises Abraham to give him the land of Canaan for his own possession. Abraham, like most of us, would have been curious as to how this would come to be: **"how am I to know that I shall possess it?"** (v. 8).

Here is God's response: **He said to him, "Bring Me a heifer three years old, a female goat three years old, a ram three years old, a turtledove, and a young pigeon." And he brought Him all these, cut them in half, and laid each half over against the other. But he did not cut the birds in half. And when birds of prey came down on the carcasses, Abram drove them away** (vv. 9–11).

In ancient culture, when two persons would enter a covenant, they would cut certain animals in half and create a pathway between the two halves. Then, they would both walk through the path together to symbolize what the covenant agreement was saying: "Let me become like these animals if I break this covenant."

However, when it is time for God and Abraham to ratify His covenant by walking the path, God puts Abraham into a deep sleep before a smoking fire pot and a flaming torch passed between these pieces (v. 17). God passed through the pieces by Himself because He was going to fulfill His promises to Abraham and the established covenant alone. The author of Hebrews recognized this great truth and writes about it in this way: **For when God made a promise to Abraham, since He had no one greater by Whom to swear, He swore by Himself, saying, "Surely I will bless you and multiply you." And thus Abraham, having patiently waited, obtained the promise. For people swear by something greater than themselves, and in all their disputes an oath is final for confirmation. So when God desired to show more convincingly to the heirs of the promise the unchangeable character of His purpose, He guaranteed it with an oath, so that by two unchangeable things, in which it is impossible for God to lie, we who have fled for refuge might have strong encouragement to hold fast to the hope set before us** (6:13–18).

If God makes a covenant with us, He does not break it. God does not abandon us, leave us, nor forsake us. You may have been abandoned by others, betrayed, and hurt, but not so with God. In Him, we can have full confidence and assurance that He is with us and for us. As Paul writes, **if we are faithless, He remains faithful—for He cannot deny Himself** (2 Timothy 2:13).

One of my favorite passages in the Old Testament, though there are many, is found in the book of Lamentations, where the prophet Jeremiah, recalling all of Israel's sufferings and woes, brings his afflictions before the Lord. Yet, despite the consequences of Israel's sins and destruction, Jeremiah bursts out into a praise well worth keeping in our hearts: **Remember my affliction and my wanderings, the wormwood and the gall! My soul continually remembers it and is bowed down within me. But this I call to mind, and therefore I have hope: The steadfast love of the LORD never ceases; His mercies never come to an end; they are new every morning; great is Your faithfulness. "The LORD is my portion," says my soul, "therefore I will hope in Him"** (Lamentations 3:19–24).

Abandonment will come in this lifetime more than once. What I can promise you is that even though we do not deserve it, those of us who have trusted in Christ and believed on God for salvation will never be abandoned by Him. Once Christ rescues us, our salvation is guaranteed and our relationship with God cannot be undone.[17]

---

[17] See 1 Peter 1:3–5.

Nothing can separate us from the love of God in Christ Jesus.[18] It is for this reason that I encourage you to lean on the Lord, pray to Him to bring faithful believers into your life, and get connected with them. And when you come across others who have suffered being abandoned, know that you now have the answer for their hurting—the gospel of grace and faithfulness. When one puts their faith in Christ, they come into fellowship with God and have a sure friend and refuge for their souls. Not only this, but when Christ adopted me into His family as a son, He joined me to what the Bible calls the "body" of Christ, that is, the people who make up the church of Christ. We join into a covenant with others who are also wed to Christ, who by their profession of faith in the Lord join God's kingdom. This is one of the blessings of gathering corporately with the body of Christ in church. We grow as a people from all different backgrounds and experiences, sharing joy in the Word of truth and growing together through our struggles and victories. There is no greater feeling than getting together with other believers and experiencing the Word and life together with those who share a love of Christ. Indeed, we find immense joy and refreshment by partaking of this blessed fellowship, and if you are one who struggles with the trauma of abandonment, I can think of no better place to be than with a group of solid believers in Christ. They will be there to encourage you, minister unto you, and share your burden with you (Galatians 6:2).

God is faithful, and His people are called to be likewise. Though with abandonment comes pain, we cling to the promise of God that He gave unto Joshua through Moses: **"Be strong and courageous. Do not fear or be in dread of them, for it is the LORD your God who goes with you. He will not leave you nor forsake you"** (Deuteronomy 31:6). Joshua was to lead Israel into the promised land which God had promised them before. This conquest would entail much conflict, warring, and bloodshed. It would involve standing up and fighting against nations who were better equipped and had greater numbers. At times, it would be a battle against impossible odds. Despite this, Joshua had a promise from the faithful God—He would neither leave

---

[18] See Romans 8:31–39.

them nor forsake them. They were going to engage in a battle for their lives, and God was with them. It is the same for every believer. We will never enter into a scenario where God will tell us that the scenario or problem is too much for Him and that we're on our own. Nothing can cause God to break the covenant that He makes with His people, and if you've truly put faith in Jesus, then you can have assurance that God is with you and will never abandon you.

ABORTION

The next traumatic issue we are going to address is that of abortion. I wanted to touch on this particular issue because there does not seem to be a large ministry for women considering abortion or post-abortion. A lot of women that I have spoken to have also had jarring experiences in the church when it is discovered that they had had an abortion in the past. This response of the church causes them to panic and flee. If they cannot find love in the house of the Lord, to where should they turn?

The issue of abortion, however, has been polarized to such extremes that it seems like to disagree with another person's stance is to entrench yourself as their eternal foe. On the one hand, there are the heralds of abortion who celebrate their decision to terminate their child as an expression of sexual freedom and bodily autonomy, while on the other hand, there are those who are staunch protectors of the unborn who could never dream of committing such an act of violence against those within the womb. Between these two camps exist an area of gray that tends to bleed into either side. I'm speaking about women who have had an abortion in the past for whatever reason, who now live with the regret of their actions because they recognize its irreversible nature. They have to decide whether they support abortion, despite the injury it dealt to their soul.

We know that trauma in any form is difficult enough, but trauma that is irrevocable—that is, an action that cannot be undone or mended to the offended party—is far more crippling. Because of this, many women who have abortions feel that they themselves must support abortion as a woman's right, lest they condemn themselves in their disapproval of it. What makes such an issue more potent is having an abortion when you genuinely believe in it, only to change your mind after it is all said and done. For those women who feel such a heavy burden for their past, they are stuck between the proverbial rock and a hard place. On the one hand, they can condemn abortion as an evil, but then, because they have committed it, they feel as though they would be calling themselves evil. But the problem goes far deeper than this. To set oneself against abortion, in the minds of those who support it, is to set oneself against them. And you may think at this juncture, "Well, if you decry abortion, you'll find good company with those who share your same mindset." And this is generally true to an extent. But I suspect that many women don't want to associate themselves with the pro-life movement out of fear of appearing hypocritical or out the fear that if it's discovered that they had an abortion, they will be judged or rejected. Maybe because of their past, they also feel unworthy to engage in the discussion. There are a number of radical groups whose message tailored around abortion is all doom and gloom. There is a lack of grace and of love, which pushes people to the opposite end of the spectrum.

Because women who have abortions cannot undo the consequence of the action (i.e.: bringing back the deceased child), the trauma takes a much deeper root than problems that are within their power to correct. However, equally true is the fact that many women who have had abortions have turned around and become defenders of the unborn because they recognize their sin. Now, at this juncture, some women reading this who have had abortion may be flinching in anticipation of an impending judgment. Let me just say in passing that while I stand with the Bible on calling abortion sin, that does not mean that your dignity as an image bearer of God has been stripped of you, nor does it mean that my heart is turned against you. I speak the truth in love with gentleness because I realize how sensitive such a topic is. Even amongst the ranks of the more radical defenders of abortion, I am confident that there are those who are playing pretend for the sake of appeasing their hurting conscience because dealing with the actual trauma of what took place is more painful than pretending to be someone or something that you are not, but truth be told, when we lay our heads down on the pillow at night, we know better. That is why self-deception is such a strange mechanism. Deception requires an object and a deceiver, and in the irrational schema of self-deception, we play both parts, because again, we would rather be anything than ourselves when our decisions carry such a crushing weight.

Before I continue on to the next part of this discussion, it may be prudent of me to establish why it is that Christians are against abortion. The essence of the issue, at least for me, comes back to who God is—a God of life. Because we live in a broken world, we recognize that some forms of violence—such as that of self-defense—are acceptable forms of violence that do not violate the character of God, for God is a defender of life and a destroyer of wicked men, which is what we regularly see in the Old Testament conquests. However, as a general rule of thumb, violence is never encouraged, and even self-defense is a response to the sin of the world—it was never naturally assumed at creation. To be sure, Adam was not sliding on his 16 oz. boxing gloves to fight against Kangaroo Jack.

Now, the crux of that argument is determined on whether a baby in the womb is a human life or not. We know that God prohibited infant sacrifice.[19] God's prohibition against child sacrifice was so strong in fact, that He repeated it over and over at different times in the Scriptures. One example comes from the book of Leviticus. We read of the Lord saying the following words: **"Say to the Israelites: 'Any Israelite or any foreigner residing in Israel who sacrifices any of his children to Moloch is to be put to death. The members of the community are to stone him. I myself will set My face against him and will cut him off from his people; for by sacrificing his children to Moloch, he has defiled My sanctuary and profaned My holy name'"** (20:2–4). If there is anything that God prioritizes, it is His name. It is His image. We need no further proof of this than to read Deuteronomy 20:7, where

---

[19] The Ammonites would sacrifice children to Moloch, a sin that God fiercely condemned and says never came to His mind for His people (Jeremiah 32:35), indicating that the depths of human wickedness in the desire to suppress the truth of God for false idols (Romans 1:18ff) is beyond mortal comprehension.

God, as part of His ten commandments, forbids the use of His name in vain. It is for this reason that some sects of faith will not use all the letters of God's name in their own literature.

The means by which the Ammonites sacrificed their children should be enough to give us pause. When the children of the Ammonite people were sacrificed, the firstborn child was placed upon a fashioned altar of Moloch. The belief was that by sacrificing the firstborn child, the posterity of the family and future kin would be secured, but the methodology employed to this end was brutal. When a family wanted to sacrifice their child, the Ammonites would super heat the altar of Moloch, which was fashioned into the form of a man with the head of a bull with a hole in his abdomen and outstretched arms which led down to the hole. Because the altar was usually metal, it would quickly absorb the heat of the fire. When hot enough, the Ammonite parents would set their child onto the outstretched hands or inside the abdominal hole and would burn the child alive.

Most rational persons would look upon this barbaric practice and ask if doing such an abominable thing is even possible. Not only was this a practice of ancient times literally, but this practice still continues today in principle. But why would the Ammonites and other religions practice such violence against their own flesh and blood? Because again, in their minds, they had something to gain from it. You see, the notion of sacrifice is rooted in the idea of giving something up now to obtain something better later. It is an exchange. A small example here would be sacrificing the pleasure of seeing a movie at the theater for the sake of saving that money for a car. While missing out on social events, I'm also preparing myself for something I feel will have more utility for me in the future than movies do now. I made sure to word that last sentence carefully, because at the end of the day, our sacrificial system is going to be based solely upon our value system. I would not forego social events for an expensive spiralizer because a spiralizer is not worth that much to me. Why is this important to point out? Because the reality is, the Ammonites were placing more value on future prosperity and blessings from Moloch than the lives of their own children. We sit and think such a practice is abhorrent, but I would be so bold to claim that many

Americans would have not only endorsed such a heinous act, but would have practiced and promoted it.

You may be challenging me at this point, but how loud is the cry from radical feminists and their ilk to approve of abortions post-birth? How many are okay with the idea of a mother giving birth to their child, only to look at it and say, "You know what, doc? Don't want it. Do with it as you will," only for the doctor to then slaughter the child where they lay? How prevalent are movements such as abortion marches, hashtags supporting abortion, and assault on individuals who decry it?

However, if children truly are considered living beings by God in the womb at the point of conception, then this means that every act of abortion inside the womb or outside the womb is an act of extreme violence against the life and dignity of another human being—it is murder. Now, I take no joy in making such a proclamation. I know many soften their words to appease the conscience of those who support or who have had abortions, but my responsibility is to speak truth in love with the sole hope of pointing you beyond yourself and your sin to someone greater, namely, Jesus Christ.

Many have tried to argue that Bible nowhere gives a clear prohibition against abortion. That is partly correct. There is, after all, no commandment that says, "Thou shalt not commit an abortion." And if I make the claim that abortion is murder from Scripture, I have to at least be able to make my case on this point, lest I fall into intellectual dishonesty. So at the very least, we will examine a few Scriptures to make the case, but better books are devoted to this topic.[20]

One of my most beloved Scriptures as it relates to life within the womb comes from the gospel of Luke. In the first chapter of Luke, we read the announcement of the coming Messiah, Jesus, and of His messenger, John the Baptist. When Jesus's mother, Mary, who is pregnant, goes to visit Elizabeth, the mother of John, who is also pregnant, we read in verse 41: **And when Elizabeth heard the greeting of Mary, the baby leaped in her womb. And Elizabeth was filled with the Holy Spirit.** This revelation takes on greater emphasis here when

---

[20] For an excellent look at the issue of abortion, see R.C. Sproul's work titled *Abortion // a rational look at an emotional issue.*

we realize that at the pronouncement of John's birth by the angel of the Lord, the angel tells John's father, Zechariah, **that your prayer has been heard, and your wife Elizabeth will bear you a son… and he will be filled with the Holy Spirit, even from his mother's womb** (see Luke 1:13–15).

There are two ways we can understand this passage. On the one hand, we can understand the angel saying that John will be filled with the Holy Spirit from his mother's womb in the sense of departure—that is—from the moment he leaves the womb. The other way to understand this is to understand it from the perspective that John will be filled with the Holy Spirit spatially—that is—in his mother's womb. However, the English Standard Version Bible from which I quoted this passage is not as clear as the Greek text actually is, for the Greek deployed here in Luke's gospel is better translated, **He will be filled with the Holy Spirit while still in his mother's womb.**[21]

The idea of the Spirit of God filling John while in the womb and John acting inside the womb indicates that John was a living being with a soul, who God fashioned and knew and had called forth according to His purposes. The same word for "filled" is both applied to John as a fetus (which is Latin for little child) and to Elizabeth, who is clearly a living being. But again, one here could state that this passage, while strongly supporting life in the womb, does not give a clear indication as to the when the Spirit came upon John. I would argue that the Greek word, *eti*, from which we derive the "while still" of Luke's text quoted above, indicates the idea of henceforth, or in other words, from now into the future, meaning that the filling of the Holy Spirit upon John would arguably be from the moment of conception, and not at a certain time in the womb, because that notion would also warrant us to ask at what point is man made in the image of God? Is it three months in the womb? Six months in the womb? At birth? And if so, what are they before these periods? After all, God seems to place emphasis on life at conception via

---

[21] For example, the NIV translates this verse as, "and he will be filled with the Holy Spirit even before he is born" while the CSB translates it as I have above.

His creative action in the world and His divine foreknowledge.[22] This is clearly seen in Psalm 139:13–16: **For You formed my inward parts; You also knitted me together in my mother's womb. I praise You, for I am fearfully and wonderfully made. Wonderful are Your works; my soul knows it very well. My frame was not hidden from You, when I was being made in secret, intricately woven in the depths of the earth. Your eyes saw my unformed substance; in Your book were written, everyone one of them, the days that were formed for me, when as yet there was none of them.** If this is true, then we can make the clear case for life beginning at conception.

For many of the women who support abortion, have had them, or plan to have them should they become pregnant, they are not unaware of this. While they may suppress the truth that their babies are in fact living, human beings, they cannot escape it. However, what is it that these women sacrifice their children for? Convenience. Pride. Their own perceived best interests. Rebellion toward God. To spite fathers. This is not to say that other women are not brought into the sphere of abortion by other avenues. The common retort against the pro-life movement is, "What about the women who were raped, or the young girls molested by their family who end up pregnant?" These, while terrible occurrences, are the exceptions to abortion experiences, not the norm. However, in the discussion of abortion, we are not looking at when abortion is acceptable by examining the way in which a woman becomes pregnant, but rather, at the nature of abortion itself. The ultimate motivation of using such an argument is simply an appeal to emotions. It is an attempt to gain an inch in hopes of then taking a mile. The problem with such argumentation is, it does not justify abortion because if life begins at conception, then the act of abortion is the unwarranted taking of that life without just cause.

In my discussions with women on the issue of abortion, I present one question that in my mind, settles the debate. "Can you give me one example wherein having an abortion is an act of justice?" When I

---

[22] See also Jeremiah 1:5, where God says of Jeremiah, "Before I formed you in the womb, I knew you, and before you were born, I consecrated you; I appointed you a prophet to the nations."

use the word justice, I am not appealing to preference. I am appealing to ethics, to righteousness, to a good and right verdict.[23] I have yet to receive a compelling answer. The truth of the matter is that the taking of a baby's life is never justice. Going back to the case of rape, when a woman is raped, who should be punished? The Christian says that the rapist—in agreement with the Scriptures—ought to be put to death.[24] However, what is the crime of the child? Their existence? What law did they break? What sanction did they violate by being born? None. Therefore, the termination of the mother's pregnancy does not solve the injustice of rape, it only exacerbates it.

I labor over this issue because it is an issue that cannot simply be overlooked or swept under the rug. In order to deal with trauma, we have to recognize it for what it is, and in the case of women who suffer the trauma of having an abortion, they must wrestle with the most painful components of abortion to heal from it, lest the reality come for them later and catch them unaware.

When we examine the trauma of abortion (or any sin), we have to rightly confess it to God because it is against God first and foremost as our Creator that our sin is against. This is why, despite David's committing adultery with Bathsheba and having her husband Uriah killed by placing him on the front lines of battle, that David can cry out in repentance, **Against You, and You only have I sinned and done this evil in Your sight** (Psalm 51:4a). It is not that David overlooked that Bathsheba and Uriah were victims of his sin, but rather, that God was the first one who was assaulted by David's actions because Bathsheba and Uriah belonged to God and were His creation before they were anything to David. So with that in mind, while we recognize the sin of abortion affects the unborn, it is a sin first and foremost against God.

Here is where the wall stands before us, blocking our way. How can we ask God for forgiveness if we cannot even forgive ourselves? The burden of abortion is real because often times, women find themselves

---

[23] I make the necessary distinction here between legality and ethics. Just because something is legal does not make it ethical. See the history of Nazi Germany on this point.

[24] See Deuteronomy 22:23–27.

wondering who their child would have been had they decided not to follow through with the abortion. Many women commit abortion with a heavy heart, knowing that what they are doing is wrong, but feeling as though they have no other options to exercise. How can women heal from this trauma?

Once we recognize what our sin is and take it to God in confession and repentance, we can begin moving forward, but only if we are able to take God at His Word. If you are a Christian who has had an abortion in the past, recognize that on the cross, Jesus paid for your sins by bearing the wrath of God for them upon Himself in your place. Paul writes, **Christ redeemed us from the curse of the law by becoming a curse for us, because as it is written, cursed is everyone who is hung on a tree** (Galatians 3:13). When we come to God in repentance and confession, we come with the understanding that we deserve to receive what Christ took for us in our place, but that this punishment was taken from us and put upon Him, so that we would be forgiven, reconciled, and free from the spiritual burdens of our sins.

When God forgives us, He is all in. God is not a foolish buyer— He knows exactly who it is and what it is that He purchased by the atonement of His Son. And when God says that the matter is settled, then it is settled. Your sin has been washed away, your guilt removed, and your soul redeemed in Jesus. When you come to God, He by no means will turn you away. The Scriptures tell us that God is compassionate and loving and is near to the broken-hearted. Trauma crushes our spirits, yet, **the LORD is near to the brokenhearted and saves the crushed in spirit** (Psalm 34:18), and, **The sacrifices of God are a broken spirit; a broken and contrite heart, O God, You will not despise** (51:17). The glory of God is expressly manifest in His mercy and grace—which He offers to us through Jesus—and it is glorious because we, as fallen persons, can never be better sinners than Christ is a Savior. After all, Christ came to die for the unrighteous to make them righteous by what He has accomplished for them, something that, they could never do for themselves.

If you have had an abortion, chances are you feel too unworthy to be saved—too lost for God to find and rescue you. Perhaps you feel that you have strayed so far that there is no longer land on the horizon of your ocean of suffering. Yet, if you do feel this way, you are in the best spot you can be in for restoration because Christ came for people like you—people who are lost and without direction, or an answer on how to right the wrongs that they committed.

Recently, I attended a small bible study wherein we were studying the gospel of Luke. We came to chapter 14 and 15, the parables of the feasts and banquets and the parables of that which was lost but then found, respectively. In these two chapters, Jesus's assertions that the least of us in this world, the guiltiest, the most wretched, the most lost, the most hopeless, and most hurting are the ones that He came to save gives us unyielding hope and comfort. This truth can easily be observed in Jesus's three parables of finding what was lost in Luke 15 with the parable of the lost sheep, the lost coin, and the prodigal son. What I find to be so fascinating in Jesus using three parables to illustrate one singular emphasis—that there is rejoicing and intentionality in God coming for and saving the lost.[25]

When we begin to trust God and His Word about ourselves and our situations, we open ourselves up to being able to see our life from a different vantage point. There is no shame, no folly, and no wrongdoing in mourning the loss of your child's life. It is in the darkest of places that we can more clearly see the light of God and His love for sinners who turn to Him. God can restore to us that which was lost. My former pastor, Ken, always used to quote to me Joel 2:25, where the Lord says, **"I will restore to you the years that the swarming locusts has eaten, the hopper, the destroyer, and the cutter, my great army, which I sent among you."**

The import of God's promise in the book of Joel would not have been missed by the Jewish people. At that time, Israel had suffered judgment from God due to their own disobedience against

---

[25] Jesus's usage of three parables to illustrate the same theme of redemption is a way to underline the importance of what He's communicating. In the Bible, there were many ways to emphasize a point. One of the ways to do this was by the device of repetition (see Genesis 22:11). Another way to emphasize importance is by prefacing your statement with a call to attention, such as Jesus saying "Truly, truly," or "Truly, I say unto you."

Him. However, God, in His mercy, promised Israel that their time of judgment was done. Israel had repented of their sins and turned back to God, and God, in lovingkindness, promised to restore them and the "years that the swarming locusts has eaten." In His blessing, God would restore the Israelites beyond that which was lost due to their disobedience. This would have been great news, because in their contrite spirit, the Israelites would have recognized their sin and their dependence on God, along with the goodness of God in not forsaking them because they were not worthy of faithfulness to begin with. It is no different for those of us who have lived our entire lives in sin before God saved us.

Found then, in the passage of Joel, is a key reminder for us to focus on what God will do and not what we have done. It is to shift our focus from ourselves to God, from the sorrows of sin to the beauty of redemption in which only Jesus can accomplish. As Paul writes in Colossians 3:1–2, **So if you have been raised with Christ, seek the things above, where Christ is, seated at the right hand of God. Set your minds on things above, not on earthly things.** When we keep our focus on ourselves and our own sin, we only tighten our grasp on the trauma we are trying to let go of. To let go of that trauma, we have to reorient our perspective by digging into God's Word and trusting it to lead us through our trauma as opposed to trying to work around it by ourselves.

What makes the trauma of abortion a bit trickier to navigate is that some women who have shared their past abortions have been promptly judged or exiled by those who should have known better. If this is your experience, let me encourage you not to simply throw your hands up and quit. Continue looking for a Bible-based church that loves Christ and clings to His Word. As stated in the section prior to this one, battles of the soul are never meant to be fought alone. The Bible places great importance on fellowship and the church of Christ acting as a body. Because of this, it is with all gentleness that I encourage you to find a biblical support group or counseling for women who have had abortions. In there, you will be able to express the situation surrounding your abortion/s, what you feel, what God says, and you'll be able to have people minister into your life in ways that this book may not be able to do. You can, like in prayer, share the innermost groaning of your heart and begin processing the deep wounds you have in an environment where you can be edified by God's compassion.

If you are not a Christian, but have had an abortion and are struggling, there is hope in Christ for you. When Jesus came in His advent, He came with the purpose of calling people to God. To reveal God. He did not come to point fingers at sinners and put His nose up at them. He did not come to throw stones. The Savior is exactly that—the Savior—and **Consequently, He is able to save to the uttermost those who draw near to God through Him, since He always lives to make intercession for them** (Hebrews 7:25). There is no sinner who God cannot nor will not save if they draw near to Christ.

One of the comforting ways in which the Bible portrays our relationship to God is akin to that of sons and daughters to their loving Father. The Scriptures tell us that God adopts us into His family when we come to Jesus in faith and repentance. Our relationship with God is not merely the relationship between King and subject, but rather, between Father and child. God's love for us is full of warmth, compassion, and goodness. If anyone understands the love of a parent, it is God, and He understands the pain that you feel for the loss of your child, and if you draw near to Him, He will comfort you. The Lord, like a loving father, will not forsake you nor abandon you because of what you have done—but will welcome you to Himself with open arms.

What I encourage women to do who have had abortions is to live in honor of their child, and to become beacons of hope for other women who may be lost and in need of Christ, who find themselves in the same shackles that Christ has freed you from. Do not live in the past that God has redeemed and use your testimony for His glory because our God is in the business of redeeming and glorifying and using the most broken of us as vessels of honor to the praise of His name. And in your tears, remember that God is with you and for you, and that **weeping may remain for a night, but rejoicing comes in the morning** (Psalm 30:5).

GUILT

Last year, I wrote a small book titled *Peter on Saturday: And the Problem of Guilt.* In this work, I labored over the life of Peter, the disciple of Jesus, because if there was anyone who would have felt the crushing pangs of guilt, it was Peter.

Guilt is a feeling that plagues most, if not all of us. We have all done something in our lives that we feel we should not have done—something that flew in the face of our most dogmatic morality. Or perhaps, we performed an action that was so outside of our character that we're still reeling from trying to figure out what we were thinking. We know that many women who have had abortions deal with a tremendous amount of guilt. The two questions we will examine in this short exposition is, what is guilt and what can I do with it?

In the human experience, we often confuse the problem of guilt feelings for objective guilt. There are times when we do something that is not inherently bad, yet we feel guilty for it—and in typical fashion, if we feel guilty, we deduce that we must be guilty. In other instances, we do something that is wrong, but have a seared conscience that feels nothing, and thus we assume since we do not feel guilty, we aren't. Both instances are steeped in error.

Guilt is, in the simplest terms, doing something we ought not to do, or not doing what we ought to do. The word ought implies a moral imperative, or in another way of saying, it is an objective statement of should. It implies that there are things we are bound to, either by self-commitment or by external authority. If I enter into an exclusively romantic relationship, then I have committed myself to fidelity and faithfulness to my partner to the exclusion of all other potential partners. If I were to flirt with another woman or engage in an action violating my commitment to my partner, then by virtue of that action, I am guilty. I have done something that assaulted the integrity of my partner and took advantage of their trust in me. At this point, I can either conceal my guilt or deal with it by being up front and honest.

However, there is another component to guilt, and it is the most important one. For guilt to be meaningful at all, there has to be an objective standard in which I can appeal to. In my conversations with my atheistic friends, I often move the discussion toward this point. In Jean-Paul Sartre's work "The Grand Inquisitor", one of the characters— Ivan Karamazov—states that *"if God does not exist, then all things are permitted."* The idea here is that if there is no divine approbation or judgment for evil deeds, then by what law should man swear to other than himself? If a man has strong sexual urges that he cannot fulfill, but finds it to be a good thing to take whatever woman appeases his eye's lust, then why should he suffer by his refrain, if there will be no law beyond himself? At this juncture, one may reply, "Well, that is why we have laws put in place to prohibit this type of evil." And to that, I would say, yes, we certainly do, however, the establishment of laws does not establish the objectivity or perfection of them, or else they would not be changing so frequently. After all, Nazi Germany had laws as well. These laws were structured to be progressively oppressive toward the Jews, and eventually led to their slaughter. Such legislature is rightly condemned, but at the time, there was a great majority of people who submitted to it. But what is the issue with Nazi Germany laws and how does this have any bearing on laws as an objective barometer for guilt now?

Nazi Germany's laws were established by men. The laws of the land are also put in place by men. Men are fallible, wicked, and prone to corruption and lining their own pockets. When men, who are the same as the rest of us, are given power over the populous, it is easy to see how that may be a recipe for disaster. This is why the United States has an intricate design of checks and balances to minimize the risk of one person or part of the system becoming too powerful, though that has certainly not stopped corrupt politicians from trying.

When man becomes the arbiter of law, it is only natural that tensions will begin to rise as different persons or parties compete for power. No further evidence of this is needed than to look at how radically different countries are from one another. In the radical middle East, women are faced with severe sexual trauma and violence as a rule of law, along with children. In North Korea, Christians are kidnapped, tortured, and murdered for their faith in Christ. Free speech is eradicated in China and freedom in and of itself has been obliterated there. Evil is rampant all over the world—a world where men decide the laws of the people. For America, less than one hundred years ago, slavery was lauded as an economic good. Blacks were seen as less than a whole person to a large portion of the states simply because the arbiter of man was man.

So the issue really boils down to this: if morality or ethics and the consequent guilt of breaking those virtues are left in the hands of man, then it is still as subjective and meaningless as if there were no laws because at the end of the day, man is no more superior to his fellow man than a square is to a circle. So guilt, if it is to be meaningful, cannot be left in the grubby hands of mankind. If man creates law, the existence of those laws does not obligate fellow man to it. All it does is spell out the consequences that will be opposed by other humans who have more power than the individual, but if that individual either expects to escape consequence (think mass shooters who commit suicide after their heinous deed) or finds the terms of that consequence to be more desirable than not committing the action, then the law is simply a plastic fence. This is not to say that laws are useless, but rather, the utility and meaning of these laws can only be as valid as the source that they are derived from—they must be defined.

And this is where God steps in. As the Creator, Orderer, and Sustainer of the universe, God has fashioned creation after Himself in the sense that all ethics reflect the nature and character of God. For example, murder is wrong because it opposes the truth of God being a life-loving and life-giving God. Anything that is evil is so because it is a want, or lack, of God, either in attribute or nature. And what makes God's law meaningful is that it is unchanging because He is unchanging.[26] However, as Immanuel Kant pointed out, ethics can only be meaningful if there is a transcendent judge who is eternal, all knowing, all good, and all powerful, or else the laws imposed could not be perfectly enforced. It also requires man to live beyond the temporal world.

So when we look at the problem of guilt, we have to look at it from

---

[26] Malachi 3:6 says, "For I the LORD do not change; therefore you, O children of Jacob, are not consumed." Likewise, the author of Hebrews tells us that, "Jesus Christ is the same yesterday and today and forever" (13:8).

an objective point of view. The truth is, all of us, in the eyes of God, are far guiltier of violating His laws then we could ever imagine. In a scathing critique of universal man, Paul writes the following in Romans 3, pulling from the Old Testament literature to make his case: **There is no one righteous, not even one. There is no one who understands; there is no one who seeks God. All have turned away; all alike have become worthless. There is no one who does what is good, not even one. Their throat is an open grave; they deceive with their tongues. Viper's venom is under their lips. Their mouth is full of cursing and bitterness. Their feet are swift to shed blood; ruin and wretchedness are in their paths, and the path of peace they have not known. There is no fear of God before their eyes** (vv. 10b–18). This kind of language is not pleasant to read because we like to think of ourselves as at least decent people. Of course, we know that we aren't perfect, but that confession actually drives Paul's point home further—if we have guilt because we cannot keep our own, imperfect moral standards, then how do we look put beside the perfect law of Almighty God? Paul's description in this light is all the more apt.

The Bible goes through great pains to establish our guilt before God because it is our guilt that emphasizes our inability to save ourselves. We are moral debtors to God without an ability to pay Him back for the crimes we have perpetuated against Him. The question we turn our attention to now is, "What can I do with my guilt?"

Remember the earlier mention of Peter? What makes Peter's account so fascinating is that it is so tragic. Peter had always been Jesus's right-hand man. He was passionate for his Lord, shared an intimate friendship with Him, and vigorously defended Jesus to the point of cutting off a soldier's ear when soldiers came to arrest Jesus in the forest of Gethsemane. Peter swore to Jesus, **"Even if I must die with You, I will not deny You"** (see Matthew 26:35). In fact, after Peter's bold declaration, all of Jesus's disciples agreed. Yet, when push came to shove and Jesus was arrested, the disciples were scattered in fear of what may become of them for their association with Jesus. Peter, on the other hand, lingered behind, trailing Jesus and the soldiers all the way to the courtyard where Christ would be mocked and beaten.

While in the courtyard, we read that Peter rejected Jesus three times when faced with accusations of being His follower, and each time, Peter's rejection became more severe to the point of invoking a curse upon himself as a way to show his repudiation of Christ (see Matthew 26:73–74). Peter, who knew who Christ was, traveled with Him for years, and lived for Him rejected and denied Christ when it mattered most. In the direst circumstances, Peter rejected God to preserve himself.

I can only imagine the agony that Peter felt when the Lord looked at him from afar after he had denied Jesus for the third and final time and what went through his mind as he wept and fled from that place where he left his Lord to die. Peter's guilt at that moment must have been tangible. The guilt of Peter's actions was the wind beneath his wings in his moment of retreat. Though it was the Lord he should have gone toward, it was the Lord that he ran from, much akin to Adam and Eve in the Garden of Eden hiding from God once they realized their nakedness after sinning. Our guilt, if left to itself, will only drive us into the dark where shame continues to grow and fester.

The only place that man can bring his guilt is to the cross of Christ because it is only at the cross that his guilt was dealt with in full. We recall the cry of David's repentance after he had Uriah killed on the front lines of battle after taking his wife and impregnating her: **"Against You only have I sinned and done what is evil in Your sight!"** (see Psalm 51:4). As king, David would rarely have to answer to anyone from a human perspective. If God did not exist, David would have lived his life guilt-free. But as a man under God's authority, David knew that no matter his rank or title, he would have to answer to God for His sins. What David knew to be true for himself is also true for you, for this is **The end of the matter; all has been heard. Fear God and keep his commandments, for this is the whole duty of man. For God will bring every deed into judgment, with every secret thing, whether good or evil** (Ecclesiastes 12:13–14).

We know that all of us stand guilty before the Lord in our sins. The Bible is clear that God's justice require that He judge sins without partiality. An infinite number of good deeds can never undo the evil that we have done. Man must be held accountable for his sins, for his guilt. If this is true—that man cannot undo his own guilt before God—then it is only logical to assert that only God can deal with our guilt, both personal and eternal.

And how scrupulous is God in His judgments? Jesus tells us that **"on the day of judgment people will give account for every careless word they speak"** (Matthew 12:36), and in the book of Jeremiah, the Lord declares, **"I the LORD search the heart and test the mind, to give every man according to his ways, according to the fruit of his deeds"** (17:10). There will be no hiding for us in the day of God's judgment. The Lord will consider every thought, every deed, every word. Nothing will escape Him. From this perspective, our guilt is compounded.

After Peter had betrayed Jesus, he went back to his old life of fishing. He tried to get by the incident and back to what was familiar to him prior to Christ. Yet, it would be during this time that Christ appeared to Peter and the other disciples on the shore, prompting Peter to jump into the sea and swim to Christ. I can imagine how big Peter's hug must have been to see his Lord resurrected—to see that he would have a chance to say sorry and spend time with his best friend.

Now, I don't know about you, but if I were Jesus, I might be inclined to knock Peter upside his head and say, "Peter! What's the matter with you? After everything I taught you, after everything I've shown you, that was how you repaid me? Are you kidding me?" I would be furious. There have been times in my life where even the slightest of betrayals ignited my temper, but betrayal to this extent? I might decide to let Peter drown in his guilt forever! But this is not the response of Jesus. Instead, Jesus restores Peter to Himself by grace and tells Peter that he is going to do work for the kingdom of God, great work, but that this work would eventually cost him his life. But Peter, after being reconciled to Christ at that moment, was a changed man. He repented of his sins and put his faith exclusively in Jesus. In that exchange, God wiped the moral debt of Peter away. It was vanquished, dealt with forever. On the cross, Jesus had made perfect atonement for Peter's sins, and what Jesus did for Peter, He can likewise do for you if you repent of your sins and believe on Christ for salvation. Come to Jesus in faith, and He will by no means turn you away. And in this coming to faith, Scripture tells us that not only is our present and past guilt removed, but all guilt forever: **There is therefore now no condemnation for those who are in Christ Jesus** (Romans 8:1). And if God says that you have been washed clean, then the debate is settled.

The gospel invites us to come to Christ freely. When Peter, by God's grace, took this invitation, God used him mightily. He penned inspired Scripture, was the first bishop of Rome, and helped grow the church throughout the known world. The man who rejected Jesus by the most emphatic means was the one that Christ used to draw others to Himself. The gospel, by eradicating the darkness of Peter's guilt, opened his heart up to the light of God's grace, and this is vitally important. You see, whether a believer or a nonbeliever, all of us who have suffered with guilt could more than likely agree that if any object depicts guilt, it would be that of a shackle, anchor, or weight. It is something that holds us back. For believers, nothing could please the devil more. He cannot obtain your soul, but he can strive to make you ineffective for the kingdom by constantly condemning you in your guilt. He can make you feel unsure of God's love for you, unworthy of fellowship with other believers, and draw you away from the Word and prayer. If you are a nonbeliever, then he can drive you further into darkness, into despair, and more than likely, into other avenues of sin as a means of numbing the pain from your guilt. These other avenues lend themselves to more guilt and further exacerbate your problems.

In John 8, Jesus tells the Pharisees that everyone who practices sin are slaves to it. If that is true, then it is also true that we are slaves to the consequences of those sins, since they exercise power over us. Guilt, being one of the penalties of sin, becomes our master because we tend to live our lives in light of it, trying to conceal it, assuage it, and justify it. We spend agonizing moment after moment replaying the instances of our guilt and even worse if we continue to engage in that which made us feel guilty in the first place! Yet, a mind of chaos in this kind of bondage is not what Christ calls us toward. A little farther down in John 8, Jesus tells the Pharisees, **"So if the Son sets you free, you will be free indeed"** (v. 36). Jesus says that if He sets a person free from sin, they will truly be free, no longer slaves to their old master, the devil. Have you ever longed for the day when you would be free of your guilt?

When I first started dating my wife, I was plagued with guilt about being in a new relationship. Every day was agonizing. At night, I longed for the day when I would be able to wake up and not feel that guilt crashing down on me. Eventually, that day came, but it took a lot of trust and grace, and a realization of the gospel's promises of freedom from slavery, sin, and death. With guilt occupying my mind, I hardly had time to think about anything else, yet, when Christ removed my guilt, I could more readily take every thought captive to obey Christ and to heed Paul's words: **whatever is true, whatever is honorable, whatever is just, whatever is pure, whatever is lovely, whatever is commendable, if there is any excellence, if there is anything worthy of praise, think about these things** (Philippians 4:8). This is not to say that there are not times when guilt from former deeds crawl into my head, but when they do, I have to remind myself that who I am is not defined by me, but by God, and if God has declared me free, then who am I to argue? Who am I to put back on the shackles that God broke for me?

Now, we recognize that the gospel is not license to sin. The gospel is not, "God freed me from all guilt, so now I can do whatever I want!" Truly, a heart like this has not been transformed by the supernatural power of God. The gospel is also not license to avoid reconciliation for guilt occurred by offense. What I mean by this is that just because God has forgiven your guilt against Him does not mean that you do not have the responsibility to go and set things right with others you have wronged. Your guilt between those whom you have transgressed still needs to be rectified in a spirit of humility and love if reconciliation is desired and/or possible. A forgiven soul is one that seeks to forgive and be forgiven. It is an accountable soul.

But what should I do if I feel guilty with a sin I've committed as a believer? First, confess it to God and repent. You may be asking, "Why do I need to confess and ask forgiveness from God if all my guilt has been dealt with?"

When Jesus's disciples wanted Jesus to teach them how to pray, Jesus gave a model prayer often referred to as the Lord's Prayer. It is found in the sixth chapter of Matthew, starting at verse nine. However, we're going to pay close attention to verse twelve. In verse twelve, Jesus models a portion of the prayer in this way: **"and forgive us our trespasses, as we also have forgiven our debtors."** Now, remember, Jesus's disciples want to know how to pray to God meaningfully. When Jesus shares this portion of the prayer, it is a model for them, not for Himself, because Jesus never sinned. In this prayer, Jesus is stressing the importance of daily confession to God. Our confessing our sin before God shows our heart toward Him and our love for Him. To use a loose analogy, I know that my wife will sin against me, and vice versa. We have chosen to love each other despite knowing this. However, when we do sin against each other, the offense is not lessened merely because we possessed the knowledge that our sinning against one another would actually occur. Knowledge of sin is not permission for sin. Therefore, when my wife comes to me and asks my forgiveness and takes accountability for her sin, it makes all the difference. It shows me that I am more important to her than being right or her pride. For believers, it is no different. We acknowledge our sins against God as they happen in our lives because we care about Him, and though God has dealt with them in the ultimate sense, it does not remove our obligation to ask forgiveness and to extend forgiveness.

The next thing we can do is confess our sins to our brothers or sisters in Christ. Many people reject the idea of public confession, but it is a biblical principle. James 5:16 says, **Therefore, confess your sins to one another and pray for one another, that you may be healed. The prayer of a righteous person has great power as it is working.** Having an accountability partner that you can confide in, or a small group of individuals that you can fellowship with is a sure way to combat sin and guilt. And gathering other peoples' perspectives in the church is an indispensable tool that many of us take for granted but given that all individuals in Jesus are referred to as the body of Christ, it only makes sense that we work in tandem.

Third, continue to be in prayer. If you still feel the lingering effects of guilt, continue to pray to the Lord and seek out His Word as it pertains to your situation. Guilt can be crippling but only if we leave it unattended. I have seen both men and women be freed from the nightmarish guilt of going through with an abortion. I have seen men redeemed from the slavery and guilt of pornography and have spoken with convicted felons who speak of their new life in Christ. What God has done for them, He can do for you. Guilt cannot withstand the light of God's grace in Christ. No amount of darkness, for even a second, can resist the light once the light comes on, and there is **In [Christ]… life, and the life was the light of men. The light shines in the darkness, and the darkness has not overcome it** (see John 1:4).

If you are dealing with guilt, take it to the cross. Take it to Jesus. He can not only heal you, but free you as well (For a more extensive look into the problem of guilt, see my book, *Peter on Saturday: and the Problem of Guilt*).

SIN

I'll never do that again.

That's what you tell yourself after committing the same sin that you've been struggling with over the past few years. In typical fashion, you offer God a quick prayer for forgiveness, almost more of a mental note than an actual prayer: "Sorry, God, that was my mistake." A few hours later, you're back into your sin, thinking, "I'm such a worthless Christian. God can't use me—if anyone knew what I do or struggle with, there would be no place for me at church and no one would want me at their Bible study. I don't know why God has saved me, or *if He even did.*"

Or maybe it's worse. Maybe you're so used to giving into your sins that you find it no longer worth confessing or fighting against. You reason that since God has seemed to clearly give up on you, why should you not give up on yourself? If in your eyes, you (wrongly) assume that God's power is insufficient to save you from your slavery to sin, then there is no chance that you would take up that burden upon yourself by your own failing strength, and that is certainly not a great place to be.

The disheartening reality that we soon discover after coming to Christ is that while we have these holy desires to do well unto our Lord, we are still able to hear the doldrums of our former life and temptations—what Scripture refers to as "the old man" or "the flesh" which resides in every believer post-conversion.[27] This can be quite maddening and guilt-inducing for obvious reasons similar to having impure thoughts about another person who is not your spouse. How could we, as redeemed creatures in Christ, supernaturally saved by the power of God's Holy Spirit with a force greater than that of creation, still fall back upon the very thing that God has saved us from?

The battle against sin cannot begin with us. Our powers are failing powers left to themselves. We are like the Greek hero of renown, Achilles—if Achilles's weakness was his heel, shin, hip, elbow, lower back, arm, neck, finger, and skull. That is to say, we are not the hero we presume ourselves to be, and that is exactly the point of the gospel, the lesson of the law, and the evidence of sin. As we will soon find out, sin is predatory. That is how the language of the Bible speaks of it in many places. But what is sin?

Elsewhere in this work, I have defined sin as a want of, an emptiness of, a lack of, God. His character, His nature, His attributions. Anything about us that does not reflect God would fall into this category of sin. Anything that is antithetical to the character or nature of God is sin. Anything that opposes God or fails to uphold His law is sin. Anything that drives us further away from God or takes precedence in our hearts over Him is sin. And even our willingness to do something that isn't sinful that we think is sinful, is sin (because we were willing to do it in spite of thinking it was an action that would displease God). Sin is a terrible thing—it is chaos and darkness.

Recently, I was reading Jordan Peterson's 12 Rules for Life: An Antidote to Chaos, and in his first rule, he talks about the Taoist symbol

---

[27] We have to be careful not to be cavalier in how we understand the text on this point, since the Greek carries more depth than its English rendering. The "old man" does not refer to age, but to that old sin nature in which we have been set free from by the cross of Christ. And the flesh, while sometimes referring to our bodies (see Luke 24:39), is primarily referencing our sinful nature (see Matthew 26:41).

many of us are familiar with: the Yin-Yang symbol. Upon explaining the symbol's meaning as being order and chaos, Peterson goes on to say that these two elements are "interchangeable" and "eternally juxtaposed" elements. That is to say, there are two parts at play that comprise the whole. The imagery of the Yin-Yang got me thinking about the spiritual reality of our lives, especially the idea of juxtaposition, which, in the Taoist formulation here, has order and chaos within the closest proximity toward one another—side by side—but also, inside of one another, represented by the one dot of the other side's color. In a loosely analogous picture, this can also be a depiction of a person's soul in the overarching picture of the spiritual battle between natures. On the side of chaos (or sin as we will use it here), there is a small white dot, which can represent the image of God in a person, though their nature is ensnared by wickedness. On the other side of order (the redeemed image), there is a small black dot, which represents the old man, or flesh. Both sides are utterly distinct from one another, yet within proximity to one another. The "order" is the Spirit of God in a person, while the "chaos" can be seen as the unredeemed world, our own sin nature, and the power of the devil.

The analogy only extends that far, however, because righteousness and wickedness are never interchangeable nor are they eternally juxtaposed. This is where the Christians differ from the Taoist and all other philosophies: **In [Jesus] was life, and that life was the light of men. That light shines in the darkness, and the darkness has not overcome it** (John 1:4–5). God's righteousness is the victory, the finale, the knockout punch against the jaw of the devil and evil forever—as Paul writes, **[God] exercised this power in Christ by raising Him from the dead and seating Him at His right hand in the heavens— far above every ruler and authority, power and dominion, and every title given, not only in this age by also in the one to come. And He subjected everything under His feet and appointed Him as head over everything for the church, which is His body, the fullness of the One who fills all things in every way** (Ephesians 1:20–23).

But here is where the Yin-Yang symbol gets it right—what is the chaos, or the black, of the Yang? A want, or lack of, the order, which is the white area (the Yin). That is why the white dot within the Yang is so crucial—it is the reason why men have not become feral beasts, fomenting disaster against fellow man at every turn, and seething at the teeth with blood lust unconditionally. It is the image of God in us, sustained by the common grace of God, not at all to be confused with innate or self-sufficient righteousness, or else it would have no need to be saved, or redeemed.

This is also why the black dot within the Yin is so essential to the believer in the sense that it tells us to never let our guard down. The proximity of the symbol's two elements is a telling one—the creeping of the chaos upon the order, waiting for its chance to strike. It is seen in the warning that God gives unto Cain: **"sin is crouching at the door. Its desire is for you, but you must rule over it"** (see Genesis 4:7), a warning that ultimately falls upon deaf ears, for just one verse later, Cain murders his brother with a rock out in the fields. For the Christian, the warning is apt. A door is a threshold wherein you go from one environment to the next. It is the distinction between inside and outside if you will. And what door is the most relevant to us? The door to our house. It is an access point, an exit point, and a symbol of our security. It is a demarcation to all others of domain, separating ours from theirs. It is, in most instances, a place of great safety for us, which is why when we see a shifty shadow or hear a strange noise from its area, we are greatly concerned. In this sense, you can consider the door to be the barrier between order (your house) and chaos (the outside world). And where is sin?

Crouching at the door.

Proximity.

Here is an interesting contrast. Sin's marching orders from its master is to go to the door of the believer, crouch, and wait for an opportune time to attack. Crouching denotes stealth. Backstabbing deals a lot more damage to the unsuspecting than trying to attack an opponent from the front who is aware of your presence. But the marching orders of the Christian is radically opposed. Speaking of the adulterous woman, Solomon says, **And now, O sons, listen to me, and do not depart from the words of my mouth. Keep your way far from her, and do not go**

near the door of her house (Proverbs 5:7–8). We are instructed here, not to approach the chaos, but to refrain from it. But we like to play the part of the fool, flirting with the taboo: **For at the window of my house I have looked out through my lattice, and I have seen among the simple, I have perceived among the youths, a young man lacking sense, passing along the street near her corner, taking the road to her house in the twilight, in the evening,** *at the time of night and darkness* (Proverbs 7:6–9; emphasis mine). The result is not pretty; I'll let you read the rest of the account on your own.

Sin is called to crouch at the door of man, but Christians are called to stay away from the door of chaos, of sin, of darkness, of irreverence. The way to approach a door is simple enough. First, there needs to be a desire to go. This desire is prompted by the thought of going, tempered through flirtation. Then, this desire needs to grow in strength so that it overpowers all other desires, especially the desire to be holy unto God. This desire, once bold enough, and accepted enough, leads to our plotting the course, so to speak, of how to get to this door. We leave the place of order (sobriety of mind, self-control), but remember, we are not alone. Who was crouching at our door? Sin. Does it violently grab us, pin us down, and force us against our will? Does it scream and snarl outside the door before we exit? No. Sin is more subtle than that. Sin waits for you to come out to play. When it sees that you have a willingness to go to the door, it takes you by the hand like a friend would and encourages you along the way. It promises you feelings of great joy and pleasure: **[The woman] seizes him and kisses him, and with bold face she says to him, "I had to offer sacrifices, and today I have paid my vows; so now I have come out to meet you, to seek you eagerly, and I have found you. I have spread my couch with coverings, colored linens from Egyptian linen; I have perfumed my bed with myrrh, aloes, and cinnamon. Come, let us take our fill of love till morning; let us delight ourselves with love. For my husband is not at home; he has gone on a long journey"** (Proverbs 7:13–19).

The woman grabs onto the young man and kisses him, sharing something that is not hers to give, nor his to take, for in this proverb, the woman is married. Then she tells him something—that she had to offer sacrifices and pay her vows. This would seem to have religious undertones pointing to temple worship and perhaps a sin sacrifice. After this, however, she tells the young man words with chilling undertones: so now I have come out to meet you, to seek you eagerly, and I have found you.

This may be a picture—not of the chaos of the woman—but the chaos of you, the reader. Have you ever been guilty of the following? Prayers of confession and penitence, all the while in your head, saying, "I'll do it again, but I have to ask forgiveness because that's what Christians are supposed to do." You go through the motions of Christendom all the while plotting to betray your Christ. I've been there and I have done that. It is a bitter reality to know it, but a worse reality to deny it because then you haven't come to grips with how terrible you actually are, and that's not good, either.

The woman then begins detailing the lengths that she has gone to for the sake of the young man. "I wanted you to have the best of the best in me." Perfumes, lavishness, silky sheets, and everything else can be worried about tomorrow morning when you wake up beside her. The temptation is in the pleasure, the enticement in the Egyptian linens, so to speak. Sin promises, and when it promises, it promises big. That is because sin is rooted in pleasure, and in the Western world, coupled with the old flesh, pleasure is the end goal of the nihilist and the greatest agent of chaos to ensnare man, because if the end that man pursues is not God, then by process of elimination, it must be himself. **If the dead are not raised, "Let us eat and drink, for tomorrow we die"** (see 1 Corinthians 15:32b). If there is no resurrection, the life we have now is the only one. What else can man search for other than pleasure if God does not exist?

We can easily, with the help of sin's persuasion, convince ourselves that what we are doing is not sinful. It might be sin when others do it, but we're the exception, not the norm. Perhaps this is why our sins are done in the dark. Or maybe behind closed doors. The point is, we rarely broadcast it—even the young man goes to the woman's house in the night hours, escaping detection from his peers. A passage from

George Orwell's classic 1984 may be apt here to demonstrate the idea I'm conveying.

Writing in his diary, the main character, Winston, recalls a time that he had had intimate relations with another woman. He lived in an oppressed dystopia under the thumb of a manipulative and tyrannical government. There was a certain type of curfew in place that if he was found breaking, would result in serious repercussions—the end of his life. He writes:

> It was three years ago. It was on a dark evening, in a narrow side street near one of the big railroad stations. She was standing near a doorway in the wall, under a street lamp that hardly gave any light. She had a young face, painted very thick. It was really the paint that appealed to me, the whiteness of it, like a mask, and the bright red lips. Party[28] women never paint their faces. There was nobody else in the street, and no telescreens. She said two dollars... I went with her through the doorway and across a backyard into a basement kitchen. There was a bed against the wall, and a lamp on the table, turned very low... She threw herself down on the bed, and at once, without any kind of preliminary, in the most coarse, horrible way you can imagine, pulled up her skirt... I turned up the lamp...

After turning up the lamp, Winston discovers that the woman is old, in terrible repairs, and has nothing but blackened gums in her mouth. White streaks of dry hair are nuzzled upon her scalp and her make-up, alluring from afar, reveals itself to be a hideous array of dry and caked application, cracking at the creases. He continues:

> When I saw her in the light she was quite an old woman, fifty years at least. But I went ahead and did it just the same.

---

[28] When Winston writes that "Party women never paint their faces," he is speaking about the Party, which was the name of the elites in the society in which he resided. It was taboo to apply make-up; Party women were aways bare.

The parallels are apparent; Winston sees an opportunity to engage the desires of his dark lusts. He sees that the woman is appealing from afar. He sees her door, and he pursues her. It is in the dark. Had there been telescreens nearby, he would most likely would have walked the other way, considering it too great a risk to indulge. Now, the formula here between Winston and the young man is strikingly similar. The shared elements between both accounts are as follows: Opportunity,[29] Desire,[30] Secrecy,[31] and Lack of Accountability.[32]

Add all of these together and sin is the inevitable result. Yet, what is the end result for both parties? The young man's fate is this: **All at once he follows her, as an ox goes to the slaughter, or as a stag is caught fast till an arrow pierces its liver; as a bird rushes into a snare; he does not know that it will cost him his life** (Proverbs 7:22–23) because **Her house is the way to Sheol, going down to the chambers of death** (v. 27).

Winston discovers, to his incredible dismay, that the woman is odious. He was duped by distance and faulty lighting and a mask of caked application. As he wrote in his diary, he had to stop multiple times, recalling the horror of his deed. He engaged a "white-washed tomb", so to speak, risking his life just to do so. But isn't that the foolishness of sin? The tragedy of human rebellion? That despite knowing how bad our actions are, we still pursue them anyhow? Why do we do this?

The short answer? Our nature. Going back to the Yin-Yang symbol, you may have observed that the sin nature in the redeemed person seems

---

[29] Note the availability of both women to the men involved in these narratives; for the young man, the adulterous woman looked for him, found him, seized him, and seduced him back to her house. For Winston, he sought after the prostitute he would be intimate with.

[30] The young man was seduced and desired to satisfy his carnal appetite by placating the sexual wants of the adulterous woman. Winston desired intimacy as a means of rebelling against his government and as a fulfillment of his lusts.

[31] The young man goes near the door of the adulteress in the concealment of night. Winston does the same to find the prostitute.

[32] The young man is told by the adulteress, "My husband is not home; he has gone on a long journey," which was just another way of saying, "We won't be caught." Winston avoids telescreens and public routes to escape the risk of execution.

to be relatively small in comparison to the whole of them, and naturally, I would be inclined to agree, but just because that torrent of chaos is small by no means dictates it to be weak. After all, how vast are the oceans of the world? Greater than we can imagine. I'd wager that you could safely swim in most waters (not including sharks, and whales, jellyfish, and the Lochness Monster), yet within these large, docile waters lie something sinister and powerful: whirlpools. These violent torrents of water can easily suck down the Michael Phelps of this world, and delights in doing so to those who believe themselves to be relatively good swimmers (sin is strongest when it catches us relying on our own strength). Something so small, yet so powerful. It even looks stunning, which has prompted some swimmers to actually approach it, leading oftentimes to their demise. Perhaps instead of saying, "Don't go near the door," we could opt to say, "Don't swim near the whirlpool." Don't flirt with chaos because chaos doesn't like to be teased. If you offer it a second of your time, with a wink, with a smile, if you have caught its attention, it's coming for you with no preservation, claws out.

This is what our primordial parents, Adam and Eve experienced in the garden. Eve saw the fruit that the serpent offered her, to make her like God, knowing good from evil (conveniently leaving out how it would occur). She looked upon the fruit and saw how it shined in the sunlight. She contemplated the words of the devil, how he promised her more than she already had. He offered her the very thing she did not have in the Garden, equality with God. And for whatever reason, she succumbed and then passed it off to her husband because all good couples share with their spouses. Sin baits, hooks, pulls, and then devours.

A few years ago, I read the story of Moses in the book of Exodus. In the second chapter, we get a story that, in my estimation, paints us a picture of sin's deadly consequences. In Egypt, the people of Israel grew to such a number as to intimidate the new Pharaoh. The new Pharaoh oppresses them with hard, manual labor of brick laying and creation. Eventually, the Pharaoh, out of scorn toward Moses's request to let the people go have a feast unto the Lord in the wilderness, decides to multiply the physical labor by removing the straw supplied to the

Israelites, but yet demanding the same amount of production from them. Do you see the problem? If I toil for all hours of the day creating bricks, and I am able to make "x" number of bricks in that time, how could I possibly create the same number of bricks if I now have less resources? It is not like the Israelites could afford to be lax in their productivity—they would be beaten for slackness—for not measuring up. So assuredly, their efforts were genuine. By removing the straw from the Israelite's supply, the Pharaoh had taken away from them, but demanded that they supply more with less. It was a progressive abuse of the Israelite. When they failed, they were beaten (see Exodus 5:14–16). The Israelites are smart enough to catch this. They basically say, "Now, wait a minute. We're getting beaten because we're not supplying the same number of bricks as before, but the conditions of the game here have changed. There's no way, Pharaoh, that we could possibly produce the same number of bricks for you. We break our backs in this labor, and now you want to take from us and demand we give you more. *How logical is that*?"

It isn't.

Pharaoh was not operating according to the laws of logic or decency—only power and demand—two potent elements of tyranny. He was unleashing chaos against the Israelites due to the uncertainty laid up in his own heart regarding them and because Moses had the audacity to make requests for their release. Power, demand, and authority are nasty things in the hand of a despot bent only on satiating his will to power. The Israelites were, in and of themselves, helpless.

If it hasn't struck you yet, this is a picture of how sin operates. It has a parasitic relationship with its host. For example, in weightlifting there is something called progressive overload, which is basically the idea that in order to stimulate growth and strength in your muscles, you have to methodically increase the stress it undergoes in new ways. This could come by increasing volume or weight or by adding more effective techniques to your training regimen. The point of progressive overload is to progress. It is to build a person up. With sin, we suffer regressive overload, where sin increases its stress upon us, to our detriment, not our growth.

You see, you're most likely aware, perhaps even intimately acquainted, with this concept. The best example is the sin of pornography. For many, like myself, it merely started with photos of women slightly indecent. But eventually, the taboo effect and the stimulus of these pictures were not enough. Sin wanted more—it was hungrier. It demanded more, and like an obedient slave, I listened. I graduated from partially indecent to indecent. Now the pictures of the women were nude. You know where this is going—but eventually I had a master's degree in all things pornographic with no diploma to show for it, but rather, a lot of guilt, shame and burden. How's that for student debt?

In his book *Closing the Window*, Tim Chester shares the testimony of a man who experienced the grueling demands of his sin. He became addicted to porn, gradually becoming more and more graphic in his searches to satiate his chaotic desires. This went on for quite some time. Eventually, he was arrested in an internet café for watching child pornography. You may think to yourself, "How could he have done that?" and it's a reasonable thought. How could anyone do that? Well, he didn't start the race there, but that's where it ended. Remember, nothing about sin is logical or reasonable. It is a game of manipulation, of evoking rebellion, and fulfilling desires in the hopes of satiating that craving for pleasure once and for all where God is removed from the equation. It didn't happen for him. It certainly won't happen for you.

This isn't the only language of doors and paths in the Bible, however. It seems to have a keen focus on the idea of them, and I believe it is due to the fact that both lead somewhere. The path is the direction with the door as the final destination. You are told not to take the path near the adulteress's house, lest she find you and kill your soul with her subtle, but not so subtle, seductions. And you're told, that if you have stumbled down the wrong path to certainly not knock upon the door, but to move away (Hint: she won't have any "No Trespasser" signs to warn you). The notorious inscription of Hell's gates mentioned in Dante's inferno, "abandon all hope, ye who enter here," sits above her door with the first five words crudely scribbled out. It's obvious what she wants, what she causes, and what her end game is, but she will do anything to pacify your conscience.

Okay, so we are told not to approach the door, and it may very well be because what lies within appeals to our old nature and can look appeasing to us. Sin approaches our door with no prohibition because sin will never be enticed by God. The unholy rebels against and despises and abhors the holy. James says that the demons know God and tremble, but they don't have faith. They have no inherent desire for Christ. Now there's a thought for consideration.

Stay away from the door because your sin was dealt with in a supernatural way. God rescued your spiritually bloated corpse from the bottom of the ocean. You were dead in sins and trespasses. It was not mere intellect that saved you, as if you were packing a suitcase for heaven and your neighbor for hell because you were spiritually smarter than he was. It was because God had, for His own purposes, chosen you as a vessel of honor unto Himself. This required a supernatural work of God to redeem and transform your spiritual condition from one of wickedness to righteousness by virtue of Christ's righteousness. By God's declaration, you were justified. This is a work of art that would have Picasso begging God to teach him how to do it. This is more powerful than Jesus raising Lazarus from the dead. Jesus raising Lazarus was a temporary fix (curbing temporal death) to an inevitable problem (the consequence of sin being death). In salvation, God provides an eternal solution to an inevitable problem, and utterly destroys it. It is not an equal contest by any means. It is Muhammad Ali battering and knocking down Cleveland Williams; Cleveland only lands a sparing few punches, but Ali destroys him with clinical precision ("He shall crush your head, and you shall strike His heel").[33] It is no contest.

If you need further proof of this, listen to what James says about the issue: **But each person is tempted when he is enticed by his own desire. Then desire when it has conceived gives birth to sin, and sin when it is fully grown brings forth death** (James 1:14–15). Our sin

---

[33] This was the punishment of the serpent after having deceived Eve; God was going to send someone to utterly destroy him. On the cross, the devil "strikes Jesus's heel" because Jesus suffers death on the cross, but Jesus crushes the serpent's head by defeating sin and death in the resurrection. In this, Jesus redeems His people from the mastery of Satan. What makes this analogy more fun is that Ali defeated Cleveland in the third round while Jesus defeated the serpent by rising on the third day.

indwells and manifests itself through our desires. This is why our call is to abstain from the door and the paths that lead to it.

But there is refuge from sin and its pernicious attacks—it is found in Jesus: **"Truly, truly, I say to you, I am the door of the sheep…. I am the door. If anyone enters by Me, he will be saved and will go in and out and find pasture"** (John 10:7, 9). Jesus markedly declares Himself as the passageway to eternal life: **"The thief comes only to steal and kill and destroy. I came that they may have life and have it abundantly. I am the good shepherd. The good shepherd lays down His life for the sheep"** (vv. 10–11). Now, juxtapose those two sentiments and the contrast could not be clearer. Sin comes to ravage its victims. Christ comes to die for His people. Which door sounds like the safer bet?

It would probably behoove me to mention here that there are only two paths and two doors that man can walk and enter: the path and door to eternal life and the path and door to eternal damnation. This is no joking matter. Jesus paints it in this way: **"Enter by the narrow gate. For the gate is wide and the way easy that leads to destruction, and those who enter by it are many. For the gate is narrow and the way is hard that leads to life, and those who find it are few"** (Matthew 7:13–14). This only reiterates the prior point that sin is natural to us, thus easy, and explains why the path to hell is so broad and popularly traversed. Compared to the road to heaven, which requires a supernatural work of God, the road to hell is one heavily—and gladly—occupied. If this is true, then this means that there is no spiritual middle ground, no opting out, no indecision. To refuse to decide is a decision in and of itself, and Paul writes that anything not done in faith is sin.[34] Your indecision regarding Christ is not something from faith. It is sinning that desires to have the appearance of neutrality and no one can really blame you for wanting to play it safe, but unfortunately for you, God is much smarter than you are, so trying to ride the fence won't do you any good, and hasn't done you any good, because sin has never done anyone any good in the history of mankind. Ever. Why do you think it would be different for you?

---

[34] Romans 14:23 says, "But whoever has doubts is condemned if he eats, because the eating is not from faith. For whatever does not proceed from faith is sin."

My former pastor Ken used to say, "You can choose your sin, but you can't choose their consequences." That's a dangerous proposition to pass between the palms. It's dangerous because it's true, and truth is more hostile to sinners than it is kind. To our chagrin, we often choose to pursue sins in a vain attempt to satisfy our incessant appetite for chaos—for defiance. To find meaning. To escape loneliness. To numb trauma. Yet, there is no light to be found in these dark depths, and we often cause ourselves to fall into deeper cycles of depravity the more we pursue them until we don't know how we got to where we currently are—all we know is that we desperately want to go back home—if God grants us the grace to even want that. The problem is that when one stays in the dark for any length of period, their eyes begin adjusting. They get used to it. They get comfortable. But at the same time, their eyes also become weaker. If you stay in the dark for too long, don't be surprised if you come out blind.

Darkness is a terrible, bitter, and savage thing, but not beyond the grace and power of God. That is the good news of the gospel—none are beyond the salvation offered through Christ.[35] Sin can only be conquered by Him who has conquered it for us in our stead. Place your faith in Christ and turn away from sin (repentance). Trust Him and His Word. To be sure, only Christ can free us from the tyrannical grip of sin. And that leads us to the next point.

If you are a believer, what I am about to say next may shock you given your current struggles. You may pick up your tomatoes, but don't throw them at me yet—hear me out. You have been totally freed from the power and mastery of sin. Sin has no true power over you except the power that you give it. No Christian can ever stand before God and tell Him, "I know I sinned, but I just couldn't help it." I would imagine that such language would only reveal a lack of faith in the power of God's Spirit.

The truth of the matter is this: we are our own greatest victims. We flirt and play with sin, put our hand near its mouth, and then become surprised when it sinks its fangs into our flesh, only to do it all over

---

[35] John 1:4–5 says, "In [Christ] was life, and the life was the light of men. The light shines in the darkness, and the darkness has not overcome it."

again ad nauseam. "I'll never watch that again," or "I'm done losing my temper with my spouse," or "I'm going to stop lying at work," becomes "I'm not harming anyone by watching this," and "She really deserved that for what she said to me," and, "If I tell the truth I could lose my job."

As a parenthetical, let me assert here what I am not saying. I am not saying that a Christian is marked by a perfect, sinless life, but rather, a markedly repentant life. As glorious as it would be to say that we will never sin again, it is not feasible this side of heaven. We sin more than we can account for. But time and time again, we repent and cling to Christ.

Now, let me make sure that what I wish to convey, I do so as emphatically as possible. Whatever I say here is also what I need to tell myself daily: you have no excuse for your sin. It has no power over you. Scratching your head yet? Do you find my statements to seem contradictory? Paradoxical, maybe? On the one hand, I say our sinning is inevitable, yet on the other, I boldly state that sin has no power over us. Both can't possibly be true, can they?

Absolutely, they can be, if rightly understood.

Let's begin with my second assertion that sin has no power over you. Paul writes in 1 Corinthians 10:13, **No temptation has overtaken you that is not common to man. God is faithful, and He will not let you be tempted beyond your ability, but with the temptation He will also provide the way of escape, that you may be able to endure it.** I love Paul's language here for one simple reason: instead of saying God provides "a way" out of temptation, Paul writes that God provides "the way" out of temptation. There is a singular, pointed, and absolute way out of our temptation. Obviously, Paul is not saying that God only provides one way leaving us searching for it like a needle in a haystack, but it is to say that God deals in absolutes, and He absolutely never leaves us hanging when it comes to escaping sin. But further than this, Paul's statement strikes me of Jesus's self-description: **"I am the Way, and the truth, and the life"** (John 14:6a). There is always a sure route out of our temptation—you are never too close to the door that you cannot turn around and run the other way. It is important to remind ourselves of this truth. We often times like to tell ourselves (at least I can speak for myself), "Look, there's no way to escape. I might as well just get it over with because I'm not strong enough to resist." Well, let me ask you this—how much effort have you given to actually resist the temptation? I'd be willing to say with the author of Hebrews, **In your struggle against sin, you have not yet resisted to the point of shedding your blood** (12:4). Jesus has. Jesus resisted constant assault from Satan in the wilderness for forty days and forty nights. His dependence was on the Word of God. Christ was so super focused on God that any temptation of the devil bounced off of Him. Satan was completely ineffective. I can only imagine how frustrating that must have been—to have the Son of God in your sights yet being unable to do anything to Him. Such is the power of God.

The first assertion, then, is a simple acknowledgment of how our desires play into our lives. Though we are given a new nature, we still fight old desires. Our old desires are akin to the sirens in Odysseus. The longer you listen to their song, the more leverage they have in drawing you to them in the hopes of devouring you. The more we listen to the song, the more danger we place ourselves in. However, if we master those desires, the chance of committing that sin is far less. Yet, to do so is much labor—more than most of us may be willing to put in without first hitting rock bottom. So while the route out of temptation may be forever present, the desire to resist our temptation is not so. That much depends on where the believer is in his or her walk with Christ. The closer we are, the less appealing sin is to us. The more distance, the closer we are to the door. There is no neutrality. In this sense, both statements mentioned above can be true without conflict.

If sin results in death and despair, it is no surprise that being ensnared in it leads to depression. One can only spend so much time in the dark before they begin to question what the light used to look like. Worse still is while we tread in darkness, we may not even know it. Sin is deceptive like that—manipulative. It can convince us that the sin we're doing is nothing more than a peccadillo or persuade us that satiating our sinful desires is much the same as indulging in a pleasurable reward. And if we begin to abstain from our known sins, we're still not out of danger, because in resisting our sin, we can also sin if we begin to take pride in our abstaining from it. Pride causes us to drop our guard, and well, that's just a recipe for disaster. We may be inclined to believe, even, that because we are abstaining from one sin, that that makes us better than our peers who perhaps still struggle with it. Sin is a nasty monster and the more we can distance ourselves from it, the better. But the question is, how can we do fight against sin when it's so prevalent in our society? If you wish to find some swords and spears in your fight against sin, continue reading. These few steps may be useful to you in fighting sin and stepping out of the darkness. By so doing, you will have gained a very necessary foothold against depression.

The first word of advice here is to relinquish any notion, thought, or idea of independence and self-sufficiency as it relates to fighting against sin. That's a tough task because if we relinquish that, then we're only left with one other alternative—I can't do this—and we aren't completely comfortable with such failure. But here's the dilemma. One, you really can't take on sin by yourself. Two, if you think you can, you've only proven the prior point. When you think that you are all that you need, you deceive yourself and make sin's job much easier. The men most swiftly defeated are the ones who underestimate their opponents. Don't believe me? How confident do you think the seemingly godman Goliath was when he came out to battle the little shepherd boy, David? Sticks and stones may break my bones, unless I'm Goliath, because then that shepherd's stone rattled my brain hard enough to kill me. Sin can do a whole lot of damage with a whole lot of nothing if we don't take it seriously. To realize this takes some time, consideration, and honesty. Become comfortable with the idea that you are not, in and of yourself, sufficient for this, and like Paul, declare, **For the sake of Christ, then, I am content with weaknesses…, For when I am weak, then I am strong** (see 2 Corinthians 12:10).[36]

If you are insufficient to the task at hand, then that means you have to take your problem elsewhere to someone who can deal with it. A sick man who gets himself up and goes to the doctor is a sick

---

[36] Paul's statement here may sound odd until you realize that Paul recognized his weakness caused him to lean upon God, and in that leaning, Paul found the strength to go on which would not have existed in himself.

man, fine, but a sick man who lays in bed until he dies is a fool. To have a problem but reject the one who can not only heal you, but supernaturally transform you, is an errand of error. The truth is, there is a person in whom you can find rest from this burden. A person who placed that burden upon Himself with no sweat of the brow and bore it. I'm talking about Christ, the same Christ who said to the thief on the cross who had earlier reviled Him, **"Truly, I say to you, today you will be with Me in paradise"** (Luke 23:43), after the thief sought forgiveness. Jesus willingly took sin to the cross, and He paid it in full. He would certainly then have no quarrels with you bringing yours to Him there! And there's no other place for you to take it. So go to God, let Him know what you're struggling with, but really take the time to analyze it. Why do you struggle with this particular sin? Where does it stem from? What causes you to desire it? Perhaps you desire pornography because you are alone and hate not having any form of intimacy, so you seek it out in illicit ways. Or perhaps you desire alcohol because it blurs the images in your mind of your abusive stepfather. Anything, even a failing liver, is better than reliving that. Maybe you snap so often because the world is simply inconvenient, and you've grown impatient. Whatever the sin and whatever its reason, explore it. This may require the help of a counselor or psychologist of sorts—there is nothing wrong with that. You wouldn't think less of yourself if a fireman pulled you out of a burning building, so don't think less of yourself because a counselor pulled you out of a collapsing mind. Your sin is a symptom most likely, and not the root. Find the root. Pull it out. Kill it.

Second, find a good support group. As much as we like to think it, we are actually not the lone wolves of the world. Your struggles are assuredly shared with others. Find them. Be transparent. You never know if someone else has the words that you need to hear to break you out of your perceived bondage and this should not be overlooked. I often find myself relieved when I can relate to others who share or shared my same burden. I think I am more relieved because I have something tangible for the weight of their affliction. I know that by my own stripes, I can help heal the stripes of others. In that way, I feel as though I am closer to the Lord, who bore my guilt and affliction in my place for me.[37] I cannot take your sin upon myself, but I can point you to the one who can. There's a great depth of meaning in that.

Third, understand the deadliness of sin. This entire portion so far has mainly been dedicated to this end. Sin has nothing to offer you, but I know that simply saying so does not rid it of its power. Just know that you, because of Jesus, actually hold the power over your sin, not by your own strength, but by His. Wield it like the sword it is and cut down every sin that stand in your way of Him. He is worthy to fight for, and He is fighting for you, as well.

The more we understand the grotesque nature of sin, the further away we will want to be from it. It is not always easy to see this, however, because the devil himself even appears as an angel of light (See 2nd Corinthians 11:14). In our tepid faith, sin's appeal is that much more. Even a plate of trash can appeal to the appetite of a starving man if he's hungry enough. Don't starve your eternal appetite by neglecting Christ only to try to fill your stomach with death. Stay away from the door.

Continuing that train of thought, our fight against sin is only going to ever be as strong as our relationship with God. This is because God is the source of our strength. Without Him, we are destined to fall, and without Him, we are not getting back up. In reality, sin is more awful than we can understand this side of heaven. Arthur Pink says,

> *"Sin is a renouncing of Him who made me. It is refusing Him His right to govern me. It is the determination to please myself; thus, it is rebellion against the Almighty. Sin is spiritual lawlessness, and utter disregard for God's authority. It is saying in my heart: I care not what God requires, I am going to have my own way; I care not what be God's claim upon me, I am going to be lord over myself. Reader, do you realize that this is how you have lived?"*[38]

---

[37] Isaiah 53:5 says of Christ, "But He was pierced for our transgressions; He was crushed for our iniquities; upon Him was the chastisement that brought us peace, and with His wounds we are healed."

[38] Arthur Pink, "Repent or Perish."

Fourth, keep your guard up. Paul refers to our battle in this world as spiritual warfare worthy of a suit of arms. The "whole armor of God" is required to resist the devil totally (Ephesians 6:10–18; you will want to pick up your Bible and read this passage). Constantly remind yourself that sin is crouching at the door. Religiously. Don't stop telling yourself this. Every time a temptation appears, tell yourself this truth. In war, you never want to have to guess where the enemy is or what they might do. Luckily for us, the Lord has provided the enemy's strategy in His Word, and we'd do well to know it. Peter says, **Beloved, I urge you as sojourners and exiles to abstain from the passions of the flesh, which wage war against your souls** (1 Peter 2:11). You don't open the gates to the kingdom when the enemy is attacking your walls. Likewise, we should never relax in our fight against sin because it certainly never relaxes in its attempts to rule over our lives. **Keep your heart with all vigilance, for from it flow the springs of life** (Proverbs 4:23) is the wisdom from the wisest man to have ever walked the planet. It is a wisdom worth etching into our hearts. We can do this by keeping our minds focused on **whatever is true, whatever is honorable, whatever is just, whatever is pure, whatever is lovely, [and] whatever is commendable** (see Philippians 4:8). A mind full of those things can scarcely consider anything else.

Fifthly, if you are in Christ, then know that your sin doesn't define you. I do not care what the sin is in your life because I know who the Savior in your life is, and if He does not look upon you with contempt and declare you a wretched sinner, it'd behoove me not to, either. When the Creator and the Sustainer of the entire universe says something, it's wise not to argue with Him. So then, what does He say about you as a believer?

You are a chosen race, a royal priesthood, a holy nation, a people for His own possession (1 Peter 2:9). You may be wondering, who is Peter writing about? He's writing about you, believer. God brought you into His people, into His kingdom, into His family. You belong to Him in ways too marvelous to comprehend. And if you are chosen for Christ, then that means that God is for you, and If God is for us, who can be against us? (see Romans 8:31ff). Furthermore, Paul writes in Ephesians

1:5, He predestined us for adoptions as sons through Jesus Christ, according to the purpose of His will. By this adoption, we have the right to call God our Father in the most familial of ways (See Romans 8:15; Galatians 4:5–7). And this divine declaration is not one that we can remove or lose because it is not one that we earn or hold onto by our own power, but rather, it is sustained by God's (see 1 Peter 1:3–5). And the love that God has for us is the same that God has for Christ (John 17:23). God's love, is of course, by extension of Himself, perfect, so that if God loves you with the same love that He has for Jesus, then you have nothing to fear because that love isn't going anywhere.[39] It certainly isn't diminishing based on your performance because nothing about God's love for you was ever determined by that in the first place, or else you'd be very, very unloved.

God is not shy about how He loves you and how He views you. It's in His Word. His faithfulness is on every page of holy writ. And if you focus on the gospel, you will see very evidently that Jesus is supremely good at saving sinners. You are no exception. Spurgeon puts it this way:

> *"Friend, dost thou think that Christ's ability to save depends upon thy fearful apprehensions of thy guilt? O soul, He is not the God of the hills only, but of the valleys also. There is no sin in the whole catalog but what the blood of Christ can wash its guilt away, and the water which flowed with the blood can take away its power over the soul. Jesus can give us the double deliverance, both from the criminality and the bondage of sin, whether the sin be of the mountain or of the valley. Only trust Him, and the dominion of sin shall be broken."[40]*

Sixth, seek to walk in obedience to God, not because you are trying to prove something or earn something, but because you love Him and that's what He calls you do, and that's what you were made for to begin with: **As obedient children, do not be conformed to the passions of**

---

[39] 1 John 4:18 says, "There is no fear in love, but perfect love casts out fear. For fear has to do with punishment, and whoever fears has not been perfected in love."
[40] "God of the Hills and God of the Valleys" (Sermon 1311, MTP 22:490)

your former ignorance, but as He who called you is holy, you also be holy in all your conduct, since it is written, "You shall be holy for I am holy" (1 Peter 1:14–16). Walking in obedience to God means obeying Him, not from a self-righteous, man-made religious manner, but from one of genuine faith. Obedience, when you break it down to its mere essence, is a translation of faith—it tells the one you're obeying, I trust you. At least, that's what it should be saying if your motive is pure. I wouldn't obey a person's shifty command if I did not trust them and was not under coercion to do so. I have to trust my doctor to take down the pills he prescribes. We obey God because we trust that God knows better than we do. To say anything else would be the epitome of arrogance. We walk according to God's law because we walk in the power of His Holy Spirit, who grants us the ability and strength to do so. And we shouldn't miss that—what God calls us to do, He likewise enables us to do by His power. Peter expounds upon this in his second epistle. As you read this, take time to wrestle with Peter's statements about the reality of the believer. In the first chapter, we read the following: **His divine power has granted to us all things that pertain to life and godliness, through the knowledge of Him who called us to His own glory and excellence, by which He has granted to us His precious and very great promises, so that through them you may become partakers of the divine nature, having escaped from the corruption that is in the world because of sinful desire** (2nd Peter 1:3–4). Peter states a grandiose truth for his readers—one that ties Christ and believer in a sacred union. Some have tried to assert that Peter is saying that we will be like God is, but this is simply logically impossible; God is eternal. By definition, as created beings, we've already lost this avenue of possibility. However, there is a notion of divinity that remains for believers. For one, we are given a new nature, a supernaturally transformative nature, which is the result of God's work. This new nature, unlike the dying world, is not transitory. It is not perishable. While our bodies die, we are going to be given a new body in accordance with our new nature. A body free from sin and death and all of its nasty cohorts. This new nature is our partaking in the divine nature, reflecting the craftsmanship of God's divine power in our souls. Those outside of Christ do perish, and they live on in the fiery torment of hell for all eternity. They die the spiritual death and believers live the spiritual life. Sin kills the soul faster than it kills the body.

This new nature is a holy nature. That is why Peter says that believers have "escaped from the corruption that is in the world because of sinful desire." We have a new nature with new desires and that's no minor detail. We've escaped the mastery and bondage of sin and given that you've read this chapter until this point, you also realize that that's quite significant!

Because this new nature is holy, Peter tells us, **For this very reason, make every effort to supplement your faith with virtue, and virtue with knowledge, and knowledge with self-control, and self-control with steadfastness, and steadfastness with godliness, and godliness with brotherly affection, and brotherly affection with love** (vv. 5–7). If you are a believer, you have the groundwork of faith—the basal presupposition that accords with your confession in Christ. Okay, so far so good. But what are you building atop of that foundation? Peter lists a host of different characteristics that we ought to strive for, but not as a buffet line where you pick the ones you like and discard the ones you do not. If God has saved us, called us, sanctified us, and redeemed us from our prior life, we ought to seek to honor that grace by obedience to Him in every way that He calls us to obedience. And this obedience produces fruit in our lives that reflect Christ in us. Paul writes of this fruit in Galatians 5:22–23: **But the fruit of the Spirit is love, joy, peace, goodness, faithfulness, gentleness, self-control; against such things there is no law.** Those sound a lot better than the rotting fruits of sin—hatred, misery, chaos, evil, infidelity, ruthlessness, and impulsivity. What we obey is what we manifest within ourselves. The more we practice walking in obedience, the better attuned to God we become, and the stronger our relationship grows. And Scripture supplies us with every tool to do this.

In R.C. Sproul's book *5 Things Every Christian Needs to Grow*, Dr. Sproul writes of five different elements in the Christian life that leads to growth: bible study, prayer, worship, service, and stewardship. While it is beyond the scope of this chapter to address these elements individually, it is worth noting that inquiry into these will provide additional growth and support in your walk with Christ, and by virtue of that, resistance against sin in your life. Remember it well—light and darkness cannot occupy the same place at the same time. Likewise, if we are walking in Christ, we cannot simultaneously walk in sin. They are mutually exclusive.

This advice is certainly not exhaustive, but I hope it is helpful. Remember that in the Christian walk, you are never alone to fight against sin. You have God and your fellow brothers and sisters in Christ. The enemy wants to isolate you—to make you feel helpless and powerless. Don't let him. When the traumas of sin rear their ugly head, remember Who leads you, what He says about you, and what He's done for you to make you His—not out of tyranny or a desire to dominate—but out of love, grace, mercy, and compassion for your soul. And remember that you were ransomed… **not with perishable things such as silver or gold, but with the precious blood of Christ, like that of a lamb without blemish or spot** (see 1 Peter 1:18–19). Christ paid for you with His very life, and when it comes to souls, God plays for keeps.

In the battle against depression, knowing that Christ is for you makes all the difference. Sin leads further into despair, but Christ is our sole hope and shield against it. When you spend time in this truth, then the healing of trauma from sin begins and continues until you find yourself becoming the one who beckons others to join you at the foot of the cross.

ABUSE

I recall as a young child the many traumas experienced throughout the entirety of my family due to alcoholism. Though I was never the recipient of any of the direct trauma, I had heard and seen enough of it to know that alcohol was no good. My experiences as a witness to the terrors of alcohol was enough for me to never want to drink for as long as I lived. It is safe to say that those who abused the bottle in my family were also abused by the bottle. Yet, as a young child, I was not all that familiar with the dynamics or the inner-workings of how alcohol worked to destroy members in my family. If there was ever a drunken argument, or remnants of violence, I'd simply sit in place, quietly observing as I played my video games or with my toys. I could not fit the element of trauma into my childish worldview where superheroes flew around in capes and everyone was good by nature.

As I grew up, the violence eventually tapered off as alcohol lost its influence over the family. In my teens, I looked back on the influence of alcohol and how it exposed me to things children should not have witnessed. Family disintegration, addiction struggles, abuses, and death were the wages of alcohol's work. I made a vow then to never allow alcohol to wreak the same havoc in my life as it did to that of my family.

Years later, I would arrive to Yuma. Shortly after, I made a friend—a vivacious and fun person full of vibrancy and youth. She had a certain flair about her and always sought-after adventure, but she unfortunately had a reputation about her. She was sexually active, and this, to her detriment. She seemed to have a loose view of sexual intimacy and the sacredness of the human body and experience, throwing caution to the wind and moving from one relationship to another in wayward fashion. Despite her lackadaisical attitude, I still wanted to help her in any way that I could to put such a life behind her because I felt that she had deserved better than this. I knew at this point, however, that men and women cannot be coerced into the kingdom. The Spirit of the Lord had to move or else the endeavor would be a dead end.

After speaking with this young girl over a length of time, I brought up the issue of her sexual background and her relational failings. She began to share her past and how it was marked by sexual assault and pain. I had suspected somewhere down the line that there was sexual trauma at play, I just wish I had been wrong. Here was a girl who had the entire world in front of her but couldn't move past the wickedness perpetrated against her in her younger years. The evil appetite of men crushed the soul of this young girl and stripped sexual intimacy of its value and worth. They assaulted her dignity, removed her esteem, and as a result, she dove headfirst into whatever it was she could find to numb the pain. Perhaps she felt that if she went into the arms of a man who cared that that would make up for the men who didn't. I don't know. I've since lost contact with her, but she comes into mind now and then.

Trauma as it relates to abuse is one that sticks. It has a certain kind of substance to it, like glue, that is difficult, if not seemingly impossible, to pry off. To remove it is to tear away a piece of yourself. It is a painful endeavor.

R.C. Sproul once remarked that defining dignity is a tough thing that many people cannot do at the drop of a hat, but that everyone knows when theirs has been assailed. When we suffer abuse, whether parental abuse, sexual abuse, or domestic abuse, there are ramifications. There are unfortunate consequences generally out of our control. For myself, I suffered forms of abuse at the hands of my older brother. Much of what has happened, and much of where my depression can be drawn back to, is from my youth. Now, my brother was not the cause of my depression, but his actions, in my estimation, exacerbated it. The insults, the isolation, the put-downs—they added up after a while. They were reinforcements to the thoughts of an already struggling mind. Speaking to him now, I know that he regrets those days of our youth deeply. The Lord has quickened his heart and has moved him in spirit to renounce such dealings with his younger brother, but the damage had been done. All we can both do is trust the Lord with it. It is, after all, because of God that my brother and I have become best friends.

Consider in your life the traumas that you suffered at the hands of another. It could be something seemingly small or something grandiose. It could be a singular event, or it could be a culmination of events over a protracted period. Whatever the case, we know that these abuses carry with them the potential of impacting us for a lifetime. If this is true, then we need to know how to look at abuse in a meaningful way that allows us to heal and move on from it, especially if that abuse has contributed or led to our depression.

The difficulty in dealing with the trauma of abuse is that it removes the autonomy of the individual who suffers it and strips them of their efficacy. It makes them feel weak or defenseless—like they do not really have control over their lives or what happens to them. It shades how they tend to view their relationships with others and influences how that person views themselves. "Maybe I'm not a good girlfriend and that's why he cheats on me," one woman may think. "My babysitter only touched me once. It's no big deal—boys are supposed to like that stuff anyhow," or, "I'll just tell my teacher that these bruises are from wrestling with my cousin—I don't want my dad to get angry if he finds out I told on him."

Abuse denigrates a person's self-image and tears the fabric of their dignity, and in an attempt to save themselves, victims may justify the offender's actions or normalize the behavior. If a person can justify another person's abuse, then they subconsciously have convinced themselves that they have the power to change that person's abusive tendencies. "I shouldn't have talked back. He wouldn't have hit me if I didn't. Next time, I won't talk back, and he won't hit me." I suspect this tactic is a desire to retain some modicum of control—a form of self-consoling that things will and can get better. Beloved, this is simply not the normative case. While we make room for exceptions and repentance, we also must be discerning and prudent to protect ourselves using every available resource we have. The Bible nowhere condones or approves of abusive behavior. We all are made in the image of God and deserve to be treated with dignity, value, and respect by virtue of the One who made us.

While it is beyond this work to catalog and assess every form of abuse, their potential impact, and the workarounds, suffice to say that if you find yourself in any sort of abusive situation to remove yourself immediately or notify someone who can assist you. The abuser has issues of their own that you cannot fix, and they themselves need help as well. There is no shame, embarrassment, or rejection to be felt if you find yourself in an abusive situation. Another person's sins are not yours to bear. As a side job, I certify individuals for becoming licensed security guards in the state of Arizona. Part of this process is by putting these individuals through a classroom instructional period where I go over the various laws pertaining to the role of an officer. To ensure success, I've also added in original content not required by the state to assist these individuals in their interactions. One of the methods that I teach them for deescalating a situation is to not become escalated yourself. Many times, people will try to get under the skin of the security guard to escalate him so that they can justify their own misbehavior. One of the ways that they attempt this is by throwing a slew of pejoratives and insults at the officer in hopes that something sticks or strikes a nerve, eliciting an equally, if not more, emotional response. I tell these new guards that they need to practice personal detachment. Part of this is to recognize that the evil and vileness that comes out of a person does not define you, it defines them. It shows what is in their heart.[41] It is the same for abuse. Abuse is a declaration of the condition of a person's soul—their lack of conformity to God's principles. It is a manifestation of sin, of tyranny, of a desire to dominate and injure. It is born of the devil: **"You are of your father the devil, and your will is to do your father's desires. He was a murderer from the beginning, and does not stand in the truth, because there is no truth in him. When he lies, he speaks out of his own character, for he is a liar and the father of lies"** (John 8:44). Those are the words of Jesus to the religious leaders who sought to kill him. They were performing the will of their spiritual father, the devil, because their desires were in line with his. Any action taken in this manner is a product of the flesh, the sinful nature. It reflects the devastating consequences of the Fall.

One character familiar with abuse is King David. When David had his watershed moment by felling the giant Goliath, it should have been the start of a great journey in bringing Israel back to where they should have been—in consistent communion and fellowship with God. In that event, God used David to save the people from the hand of the Philistines. David gained renown and the attention of the king, King Saul, who himself was too afraid to accept Goliath's challenge to fight him one-on-one (1 Samuel 17:11). When David slays Goliath with nothing more than a slingshot, Saul is awestruck. He recruits David and keeps him by his side (18:2). David finds much success and proves himself to be an outstanding soldier for Israel and Saul, gaining a reputation and a high rank in king Saul's military. However, the story quickly takes a turn for the worst. Shortly after Saul's

---

[41] See Jesus's teaching on this point in Matthew 15:10–11.

celebration of David, we read that Saul's jealousy is quickly kindled by the people's reception of David more than their reception of Saul: **As they danced, they sang: "Saul has slain his thousands, and David his tens of thousands"** (v. 7). Saul is fuming. With David gaining so much notoriety, what was the point of being a king? Saul's heart should have been to please God, but it was more focused on the worship of man. From this point on, Saul, who at first loved David, subjected David to mental and physical abuse. He would try to kill David with a spear. He would try to manipulate David into marrying his daughters as to get David to prove himself by slaying many Philistines in the hopes that he would die in battle. He chased David all over with his armies in an attempt to find and kill him. David was suffering great tumult by the hand of his king, and many of David's emotional responses we find in the Psalms, detailing just how downtrodden he was in spirit. To David, it felt like the world was ending. It felt like the enemy was winning. It felt like the world was collapsing, but David had something that Saul did not. David had the Lord. David had the love and grace and protection of God. Despite David being stuck in the wilderness, he was richer than king Saul could have ever dreamed of being. And eventually, David becomes the king over Israel. Throughout the abuse that David suffered, he clung desperately to God:

> *I lift up my eyes to the hills.*
> *From whence shall come my help?*
> *My help comes from the* LORD,
> *Who made heaven and earth.*
>
> *He will not let your foot be moved;*
> *He who keeps you will not slumber.*
> *Behold, He who keeps Israel*
> *will neither slumber nor sleep.*
>
> *The* LORD *is your keeper;*
> *the* LORD *is your shade on your*
> *right hand.*

The sun shall not strike you by
day,
nor the moon by night.

The LORD will keep you from all
evil;
He will keep your life.
The LORD will keep
your going out and your coming in
from this time forth and
forevermore. (Psalm 121:1–8)

I bless the LORD who gives me
counsel;
in the night also my heart
instructs me.
I have set the LORD always before me;
because He is at my right hand, I
shall not be shaken. (Psalm 16:7–8)

You cannot go through the Psalms without seeing just how much David suffered. Despite this suffering, David always found comfort in God, and that is what we aim to do when we suffer at the hands of another because we know that God will not overlook injustices in this world. There will come a day when all have to give an account of their lives before the Lord, and on that day, recompense will be made for all evil perpetrated by man against man. No sin will be hidden from God's sight.

If you find yourself depressed from prior abuse, do not feel ashamed or weak. Traumatic events are burdensome and weary the soul. You were the victim of an evil person; what you need is healing, perspective, and support. You need a chance to express yourself, to talk about your experiences and to find a way forward. In Christ, we can find healing for every burdensome wound and pain: **"Come to me, all you who are weary and burdened, and I will give you rest. Take my yokes upon you and learn from Me, for I am gentle and humble in heart, and you will**

find rest for your souls. For My yokes is easy and my burden is light" (Matthew 11:28–30). Do you hear Jesus's call? Jesus calls us to find rest and reprieve. To Him we can carry our woes and our pains. He cares. He listens. He understands. The God-man who suffered the worst abuse by man is not indifferent to your suffering, beloved. He wants you to cast those heavy chains off of your shoulders onto Him. He can carry it. He can deal with it. He can free you and He can heal you. He can restore your broken heart, wipe your tears, and console you: **[God] heals the brokenhearted and binds up their wounds. He determines the number of the stars; He gives to all of them their names** (Psalm 147:3–4). The God of the universe who knows every star by name knows you. **"So do not fear, for I am with you; do not be dismayed, for I am your God. I will strengthen you and help you; I will uphold you with My righteous right hand"** (Isaiah 41:10). Seek after God, that like David, you can say, **"LORD my God, I called to you for help, and You healed me"** (Psalm 30:2). The Lord will by no means turn you away when you come to Him. Consider Jesus's ministry. To whom did Christ come? Was it not for the least of us? The sick, the destitute, the maimed, the diseased, the lost, the hopeless? When we look at Jesus's ministry, Jesus had a deep compassion for widows. He had a heart for the children, for the lepers, for the blind, for the sinful, for the shamed. He cast no aspersions at any who came to Him in faith but took them into His arms without a second's thought. This point was illustrated in a sermon by R.C. Sproul in his sermon on reading the Bible existentially:

> *"Even go from the Old Testament to the New and think of the drama that surrounds Jesus's ministry to the leper. How the leper comes down the street and sees Jesus, and he cries out in a loud voice, "Jesus! Have mercy upon me!" And that wretched man is begging on the street and Jesus walks over and breaks all the laws that are set forth here about contamination and contact with somebody involved with the scourge of leprosy—Jesus comes over and touches him! What does that say to you about your Lord? Who will stoop down from His throne on heaven and place His hands on the most wretched flesh of mankind to bring healing to a human life."*

Jesus condescended to bring healing and life and reconciliation to God. He can bring healing to you from the abuse that you suffered. He can bring freedom to the chains that bind you, if you will but come to Him in faith, casting yourself and all of your sorrows at His feet. The Lord will not turn you away.

The healing hand of Jesus was demonstrated powerfully to me through the testimony of another woman I had known as a young child. We called her sister Hope. Hope shared her story with us one day, detailing how as a young girl, she was sexually abused by her uncle for years until it was eventually found out. The uncle was excommunicated from the family and Hope was left to try to piece her life back together—to try to put the fragments of her soul in proper order. She couldn't do it. After suffering the loss of her innocence, she felt dirty, used, and discarded. She felt worthless. Later on, Christ found her and ransomed her. He saved her and began the healing process. After a few years, sister Hope attended a family reunion. Everything was going smoothly, until to the dismay of everyone there, Hope's uncle showed up. The family was outraged. How could this man who violated his own niece dare to show up at a family reunion? Did he lose all sensibility?

The family began to ask around, trying to figure out who invited him. When Hope heard the commotion, she gathered everyone's attention and said, "I know you are all wondering who invited him here, but I want you to know it was me. I invited him here because I forgave him because Jesus forgave me."

It was a powerful statement. Hope clung to Jesus, found healing for her soul, and through it, the freeing power of Christ's forgiveness. She opted for mercy, for reconciliation, for joy over despair. I never heard what became of her uncle—I can only hope he turned his life over to Christ. I suspect that from this powerful display of forgiveness, Christ most likely took a hold of his heart and saved him.

Hope's story is one of inspiration. It doesn't mean that we have to go and invite our abusers to our family reunions. Indeed, we aim to protect ourselves from those who perpetrated such crimes against us, all the while, by the grace of God, praying that God removes the hurt from our soul and saves that individual from their sins. We pray for forgiveness to operate in our heart because we recognize the weight that has been lifted from us by Christ offering forgiveness for our sins. When we look through the lens of the gospel, even the most heinous abuse holds no power over us. We may hurt, we may cry, and we may not fully understand, but we can trust that God knows what He is doing. Pray to the Lord. Find a strong, gospel-oriented church. Get involved in support groups. Use your testimony of God's grace to those who might be in the shoes you used to wear. And if you are still in an abusive situation, it is my prayer that you find refuge, protection, and help.[42] And always remember, the God who knows the stars by name has not forgotten you.

---

[42] For the national domestic abuse hotline, call 1-800-799-7233 or visit thehotline. org for more information and resources. For women suffering domestic abuse, there are usually battered women's shelters that operate locally. Reach out and partner with any church you are associated with. If possible, remove yourself from the abusive environment. You are not bound to an abusive partner. Separate yourself and seek out assistance from the law and ensure your own safety.

5

Of a Rain that Never Stops

Somewhat troubling about depression and suffering in this life is that we never know when it will end—we never know if it will get worse before it gets better—if it gets better at all. That's quite troubling because we're not long for the miseries that this world so eagerly heaves upon us. We're short-sufferers, which I believe explains why the Scriptures call us to endurance time and time again. Not only does the Bible call us to endurance, but it also gives us an encouragement in it: **My brethren, count it all joy when you fall into various trials, knowing that the testing of your faith produces patience. But let patience have its perfect work, that you may be perfect and complete, lacking nothing** (James 1:2–4).

It may seem like an odd exhortation to call people to joy amidst their suffering. I've never suffered from a sickness and found myself tempted to dance in celebration because of it. All I wanted to do was get through the suffering as fast as possible, not endure it. But often times in our suffering, we have no choice but to endure because it is usually external circumstances that bring about our suffering. That's not to absolve man of his responsibility or to feed into the victim culture so prevalent in our day and age. Fools eat the fruit of the garden they never planted, so to speak, and so starve to death on account of their lack, but what of the diligent man who falls ill with cancer? An unwelcome scenario for all who suffer it, yet the scenario they must face, nonetheless. What joy could there possibly be in such a miserable happenstance as that? Or of the loss of a loved one? Or of being destitute?

The uncertainty surrounding suffering only exacerbates its effects on the body and soul. My car breaks down. Okay, not so bad. Maybe it's a simple fix. Wrong. The transmission blew out. Well, the average cost of fixing a transmission isn't exactly dollars and pennies, so the stress of that cost builds up. I can cover it, however. Wait—no, I can't. Rent was just taken out of my account this morning. On the bright side, I now have enough money for some groceries since I don't have to worry about putting gas in my car. But if I don't have a car, I don't have a ride to work. Well, that's no good because I already called out last week to help my dying uncle. Great. Can I afford an Uber? What if I siphon the gas from my car when the tow truck driver isn't looking? This isn't good. My wife told me that if I didn't get my act together that she's going to take our daughter and leave. My daughter! I totally forgot I was supposed to pick her up today. Okay, it's understandable, I'll just call my wife and tell her... no, I won't. Phone battery is dead. Tow truck driver apparently still lives in 1920 because he looks puzzled when I ask him to borrow his cell phone. Now what's going to happen? This is the worst day of my life.

One single incident of suffering produces a tidal wave of misery—all events connected in some way to all the others—which cascades down all at once. Now the suffering affects the realm of transportation, finances, career, and family—all from one blown transmission. In other words, suffering is a stock that is easily accumulated, but has no return on investment. This kind of suffering contributes to extreme bouts of anxiety and stress, which negatively impacts a person's entire being. Are we really to count it all joy to suffer? Why can't the suffering just stop? Unfortunately, we live in a broken, sinful world, and the consequences (or wages) of sin is death (Romans 6:23). So even if we're not experiencing suffering at the moment, it is a sure thing that suffering of some sort is coming our way at 100 miles per hour.

Some may look at this passage sideways. Outside of its context, this is understandable. Perhaps it's because in today's modern vernacular, we tend to understand joy and happiness as being synonymous. This couldn't be further from the truth. When we speak of happiness, we speak of that emotion that is elicited when things go the way we want, or when we experience some kind of boon. That is as far as it goes. It's a shallow, temporary emotion that is perhaps the most fragile emotion of the human experience. It is hard to obtain, but easily lost. For example, you meet someone whom you find yourself romantically interested in. You tell your family. Your friends hear all about this person for two weeks (much to their chagrin). Then the date is set for you two to finally meet. You're happy and excited and all of the other things that people are when they walk into the room expecting their Romeo or Juliet. But then within five minutes of talking regret sets in. This person is rude, obnoxious, and can't help but interrupt you every other sentence. Now You're angry, but also embarrassed and slightly humiliated. You thought this person might give you a chance at a serious, romantic endeavor. Needless to say, there's no second date.

Happy in one moment, depressed five minutes later and full of dread that you have to finish your meal. That's the underwhelming power of happiness. But happiness and joy are not the same thing because happiness is reactive and solely emotive. Joy, as we see it presented in the Scriptures, has to do with a state of mind and deliberate response to all things, adversity included. Because joy encompasses all situations of the human experience, it is a hallmark of the Christian life and part of the list of fruit that embodies the Christian persona (see Galatians 5:22–23).

Let's go back to James. Who was his audience? Contextually, scholars date the epistle of James from as early as 45 AD to around 60 AD, but before 62 AD when he was martyred. For those unfamiliar with Christianity, it wasn't a very well-liked faith. In the eastern world, the prominent system of belief surrounding the Jewish people were polytheistic. The Greeks had their pantheon of gods, the Romans, theirs. Even Cesar himself was regarded as a deity amongst men, requiring tribute to be paid to him. The Romans and Greeks certainly didn't mind other people practicing their religion so long as it did not conflict or exclude theirs. As I've heard one person say, the gods to the Greeks and Romans were like trading cards to young kids. Everyone had them and were willing to share them. But this isn't what the Jews did. They were monotheists who believed in one God, Yahweh, who the Romans let practice their religion in isolation for the most part, so long as they behaved and paid taxes. So while the Jews and Romans were not the best of friends, they tolerated each other well enough. Well then, you have the Christians who are an odd sort of group because they're not playing by the rules of the Jews or the Romans. To the Jews, they're saying, "You've got the instructions to the game, but you don't understand them," and to the Romans, they're saying, "All of your cards are inferior counterfeits." They do this by professing faith in Jesus Christ, who they claim (rightfully) is God in the flesh, the Son, second Person of the Trinity, incarnate. They refuse to acknowledge Cesar as lord, they reject the pantheon of all other gods, and mark out faith in Christ as the sole and exclusive way to have a right standing with God. This sounds like something the Jews would go for on the surface, but the Jews seem to be more venomous and vindictive than the Romans! They didn't particularly like Jesus because He wasn't the Messiah they were expecting. They also wanted to kill Him because they understood that He claimed to be God and that was blasphemy worthy of death. He also called them out on their wickedness and hypocrisy and thwarted every one of their attempts to ensnare Him in some contrived scandal. Needless to say, if you're talking in a room and not making friends, you're probably making enemies; this was the result of Christianity. Those who believed did so by the supernatural power of God's Spirit, drawn in by efficacious grace alone, while those who rejected the gospel of Christ became further hardened in their hearts against it. Truly, the Word of God is rightly called a double-edged sword (Hebrews 4:12). But those who despised and rejected Jesus did so by the most emphatic means possible. This visceral response inevitably led to a long stretch of persecution and tribulation for the early church which lasted for over 300 years. Because of this, a lot of believers lost everything. Many lost their homes, their connections to their family, their resources, their safety, security, and ultimately, their lives. It was a time of harrowing and unforgiving circumstances. To believe in Christ was a radical and oft bloody affair rife with death. It is to this sort of audience that James is writing to count all trials and suffering as joy.

Now, if life was truly only in the here and now, this kind of exhortation would be the ramblings of a madman, but when James writes to the church, he's writing to Jews who are suffering for a reason. They're suffering for their profession of faith in Jesus, a profession that saved their souls from eternal damnation in the hell of fire. They've been reconciled to their God by the blood of their Lord shed at Calvary. The price of salvation was steep indeed.

If the church is suffering for their faith in Jesus, then their reward is already set in heaven for them. In light of eternity, the suffering they were to face would be but a breath. But there is a grander point to be made here: our suffering is not arbitrary. I touch more on this in the proceeding chapter, but suffice to say, our suffering is not outside the sovereignty of God. God is powerful beyond our comprehension. He uses our suffering for our benefit and His glory. Often times, our suffering is a wake-up call to us that we've spent too much time depending on ourselves. So in the context of persecution, believers could rejoice because they knew that they were suffering with their master, Jesus Christ. Interestingly enough, Jesus foretold of such occurrences (see John 15:18–21) and tells His disciples that if they do not bear their cross for the sake of Christ, that they are not worthy to be His disciples (Luke 14:27). The Christian life then, is in one sense a call to suffering, but in another sense, a call to freedom from suffering—especially the freedom from the power that suffering tends to exercise over us.

I've noticed in my short tenure upon this world that suffering has the innate power to shape worldviews. Heartbreak turns Romeo into a monster. Death of a loved one makes one afraid of getting close to others, lest they lose them as well. Childhood abuse leaves one with the conclusion that God's not real. Another person loses their job and throws themselves off the bridge believing they have nothing left to live for. Whether we like it or not, suffering affects us in more ways than just one. For the Christian, suffering may convince a person that God is angry with them or has abandoned them.

Now, I'm not God, and I won't act as if I know the mind of God. We know from Scripture that God does punish people on earth—that much is clear. We also know that at times, as a loving father does, God disciplines and chastises His children. After all, **he who spares the rod hates his son** (Proverbs 13:24a). But when God disciplines His people, He does so out of love. When people experience suffering, they tend to believe God is targeting them specifically, and that He hates them or acts out of malevolence toward them. That is a misapprehension of the utility of discipline.

We also know from Scripture that suffering is a natural result of the Fall and the consequence of living in a sinful, fallen world. The grace of God, then, is manifested in how He uses this suffering to His own glory, as in the case of the man born blind in John 9: **As [Jesus] passed by, He saw a man blind from birth. And His disciples asked Him, "Rabbi, who sinned, this man or his parents, that he was born blind?"** (vv. 1–2).

The conclusion drawn by the disciples was that the man had an ailment from birth because either he or his parents had sinned. The nature of the sin was also assumed to be grievous; the fact that the disciples could connect the parents' sin to the blindness of their son demonstrates this. Jesus dismisses this errant interpretation (and that serves as a warning for us not to overreach in our assuming why things happen the way that they do). He corrects them by saying, **"It was not that this man sinned, or his parents, but that the works of God might be displayed in him"** (v. 3). God had His purpose in this blind man's malady in that he was to be a recipient of grace who would testify to the person and work of Christ by virtue of his healing. God is not obligated to heal us because the wages of sin are rightfully earned by us and the pain we feel now is certainly a grace in light of the judgment we deserve. So, we are never truly suffering as we ought to be, but God is gracious and forebears our sins that we may come to His Son for forgiveness and reconciliation.

All of this to say, that at times it was most likely a tempting thought to believe that God had abandoned His people over to persecution and suffering. James wanted them to see beyond the temporal to the eternal. He wanted them to see that suffering was within the control and power of God, and that God could use it for good. The persecution would produce patience and build up the church, and we know this to be true because every time the church is attacked, it grows exponentially. This is what is happening in the Middle East and in China.

Ultimately, James wanted the people of God to see that God was with them in their sufferings. He had not abandoned them. And it's absolutely true that suffering builds character if again, it is understood in the right light. I can rejoice in suffering knowing that it is in the hands of a good God, and that I am being fashioned into the image of Christ. I can rejoice in my suffering knowing that I'm not alone, and when I close my eyes for the final time, I will be with the Lord in heaven where pain and death and suffering are no more. That doesn't mean the suffering hurts less in this life. It doesn't mean that the problem of depression simply vanishes into thin air, but what it does mean is that in spite of these things, I still have hope—an anchor within the soul (Hebrews 6:17–20).

Paul and Peter both echo the same sentiment as James. Paul, in Romans 5, writes, **Therefore, since we have been justified by faith, we have peace with God through our Lord Jesus Christ. Through Him, we have also obtained access by faith into this grace by which we stand, and we rejoice in hope of the glory of God. Not only that, but we rejoice in our sufferings, knowing that suffering produces endurance, and endurance produces character, and character produces hope, and hope does not put us to shame, because God's love has been poured into our hearts through the Holy Spirit who has been given to us** (vv. 1–5). Peter likewise writes in his first epistle; **Blessed be the God and Father of our Lord Jesus Christ! According to His great mercy, He has caused us to be born again to a living hope through the resurrection of the dead, to an inheritance that is imperishable, undefiled, and unfading, kept in heaven for you, who by God's power are being guarded through faith for a salvation ready to be revealed in the last time. In this you rejoice, though now for a**

little while, if necessary, you have been grieved by various trials, so
that the tested genuineness of your faith—more precious than gold
that perishes though it is tested by fire—may be found to result in
the praise and glory and honor at the revelation of Jesus Christ (1
Peter 1:3–7). It may be easy to miss the parallel at first glance, but see
how both Paul and Peter preface their statements about suffering and
rejoicing with the glorious truths of the gospel hope they have in Christ?
The gospel is the lens through which the Christian is to interpret his
suffering according to the will of God. When believers look through
the right lens, they see a clear image. All of those outside of Christ
can only see suffering as a meaningless and arbitrary experience that
has no ramifications. We have no hope through it, no justification for
it, and no answer to it. We endure one suffering only to come into the
next. But for the Christian, every moment is cause for rejoicing because
of what Christ accomplished for us on the cross. There, He took the
ultimate suffering—bearing the wrath of God—in our place. Surely
then, the sufferings that go for eternity eclipse the mere temporal
sufferings of this world. And if that is the case, then how much more
does the eternal life we have in Jesus eclipse our suffering? Paul puts
it this way:

> *Since we have the same spirit of faith according to what has*
> *been written, "I believed, and so I spoke," we also believe,*
> *and so we also speak, knowing that He who raised the*
> *Lord Jesus will raise us also with Jesus and bring us with*
> *you into His presence. For it is all for your sake, so that as*
> *grace extends to more and more people it may also increase*
> *thanksgiving, to the glory of God. So we do not lose heart.*
> *Though our outer self is wasting away, our inner self is being*
> *renewed day by day. For this light momentary affliction*
> *is preparing for us an eternal weight of glory beyond all*
> *comparison, as we look not to the things that are seen but to*
> *the things that are unseen. For the things that are seen are*
> *transient, but the things that are unseen are eternal.* (2nd
> Corinthians 4:13–18)

There is a distinct beauty in the way that Paul understands suffering as a light and momentary affliction preparing us for an eternal weight of glory. Somehow, all suffering we endure on this earth is to our benefit. We live in a world where sin and death sow and reap disaster, but even as terrible as they are, God can use them to His glory and our good. I explore this idea in more depth in the final chapter of this book, but it will suffice to say here that our suffering, whether long or short, is being used by God for His kingdom and our growth.

You may be suffering. Chances are, there's something going on in your life causing you great distress. Something that continues to push your depression further. Can I just ask you to close your eyes and take a breath? It's going to be okay. You're going to be okay. It all works out in the end—according to His will. We are not always called to understand, but we're always called to trust. When you place your trust in Christ, understanding that He bore the suffering that His people deserved and believe in Him for eternal life, then you have peace with God and freedom from the power of suffering and depression; then you are able to find the same inward renewal that Paul speaks about, though your outer-self wastes away.

Suffering in this life is inevitable, but it is not forever. There will come a time when God rights every wrong, wipes every tear, and destroys sin and death forever, giving His people peace forevermore (see Revelation 21:4). A time when we can be in the perfect presence of our Lord who came to call sinners to Himself through His atoning sacrifice (Mark 2:17). And despite suffering in this life, we are never alone.

In John 16, Jesus is telling His disciples about His departure. Naturally, they are a bit confused and upset about this news. Jesus encourages them and tells them that He must go so that He can send the Spirit, whom Christ calls the Helper, who will be with every believer, providing truth and comfort to them (John 16:5–7). Christ speaks of the Spirit as Helper earlier in John's gospel as well (John 14:16, 26; 15:26). The King James Version of the Bible translates the Greek word *parakletos* as Comforter—one who aids us and is with us (The prefix "para" means next to or side-by-side). The Spirit lives within believers, guides them, convicts them, conforms them to Christ, sanctifies them, and comforts them in their sorrows and tribulations, reminding them to not lose hope. For as Christ Himself said to His disciples, **"I have said these things to you, that in Me you may have peace. In the world you will have tribulation. But take heart; I have overcome the world"** (John 16:33), so too does the Spirit testify.

Take heart in Christ, beloved. Though your suffering in this world may be long, Christ has overcome it.

PERSONAL APPLICATION

I can recall in my own life struggling with endurance. When you have depression, each day can be a monumental battle. Many people underestimate just how powerful depression's grasp can be on a person. When I first encountered it, it was enough to make me want to go into the kitchen and grab hold of a knife. It's a bottomless feeling both in mind and stomach. What makes matters worse is the fact that suffering is a slow endeavor. Even when the pain is brief, the length of it feels longer than it is. I experience this phenomenon every time I enter the weight room. The burning that only lasts for five seconds feels like a lifetime during the exercise. The one-minute break in between sets feels like ten seconds. To be sure, suffering and bliss don't follow the same clock.

Perhaps the worst bout of lengthy suffering occurred when I lived in Phoenix. Shortly before I moved, my wife and began to talk. When things started to become more serious, I began to be filled with serious dread and guilt about being in a new relationship having been divorced prior. Despite knowing better, I felt as though past baggage and hurts meant that I still had some attachment to the past. The realization that I had shared intimacy with someone else other than Jen plagued me. I felt like I had given something up that I should have saved for her. I felt dirty and ashamed of my sexual past, scourged myself every time I could remember anything from it, and condescended myself time and time again, telling myself I was a bad boyfriend. Each day, I lived with this crippling guilt which only exacerbated my depression. Every time I spoke with Jen, I felt like a liar wearing two faces. The more I tried to mentally escape it, the more time I spent with it mentally. I scoured the internet to see if this was a natural occurrence for people previously divorced and this seemed to be the case. But even knowing this, I couldn't get rid of the guilt feelings. It was a constant tension, tearing at both mind and heart. I'd go into such deep depressions, feeling like the nightmare would never end. Time and time again I'd vent to Jen and to others about my problem and everyone would assure me nothing was wrong and that I was overthinking it. Sometimes, I felt as though my depression had a life of its own, and it was doing its very best to ruin mine.

This deep agony led me to isolate myself. It was affecting my work. I'd find myself so down in the dumps that to focus on my work was impossible. Suicidal thoughts became a strange normative for me. Then one day, my boss called me. He must have been able to tell that something was wrong because he asked me, "Is everything okay?" That question—that simple, yet pointed question. It's almost like a trap. People ask it, sometimes in the form of, "How's everything going?" or "How are you doing?" We all lie. We're all apparently doing great, and the family is happy, and we're on top of everything with smiles plastered on our faces. Look at the sad state of the world. If this is everyone at their best, I shudder to think of what we'd be if we were anything less. But the truth is, we lie. We play games, we live facades. Why? Simply put, we don't want to look like the weakest link. We don't want to be the guy or gal whose marriage is falling apart for the third month in a row, or whose wayward son ran a little farther from home. We want to look like we have it all together. Is it pride? Saving face? Who knows? Whatever the case, we generally are good at giving the same response of, "I'm good! How are you?" And why wouldn't we? What would be the expression on someone's face if I said, "Well, truth be told I've struggled with suicidal depression for fourteen years, and two days ago, I was struggling to get rid of those thoughts. How are you doing?" But sometimes, you can tell when someone is genuinely asking. And it makes you think about how you really are. And you'd feel awful lying to someone who was really trying to know because they cared about you. So after a pause, eyes growing hot, I said, "No, not really. I've been having a lot of thoughts about hurting myself, and I'm not really sure I want to be here anymore."

That conversation caused us to meet in person. I broke down in front of my boss like a child and laid it all out on the table. He shared his own battle with depression with me and encouraged me to see a counselor. He gave me a hug and told me everything was going to be okay and that he had my back. That was monumental.

As I continued to struggle, I wondered why God would let me undergo such torment. Was I wrong to ask God, "Why?" Was it sinful to request relief from my mental ailing? I don't believe so; I believe to want to be rid of suffering—to have that basal understanding that pain and depression was not part of the original blueprint—was not in and of itself a sin. I didn't blame God; I just desperately wanted His help. Who wouldn't? Every morning, my first thought was about the same issue and every night, my last thought was similar. Don't even get me started on all the thoughts in between.

What got me through it? Well, first and foremost, God's grace. Without the Spirit of God, M.R. Scott ceases to be. I wouldn't have had the strength to carry on to where I am today. Keeping in mind the two crucial passages of Scripture that should be in the arsenal of every Christian (I'm speaking about Romans 8:28 and 1 Peter 5:6–7), I always had a place of refuge in God's truth that I could flee to in moments of deep despair. That was everything. But there was also something else that got me through long bouts of suffering. It was the realization that at some point, the things that bothered me would no longer be an issue—that eventually, I would get over it and get on with my life. It's akin to waiting for a cut to heal. I don't pretend like the cut never happened, but I also know that at some point, the wound will heal.

When I lived in Pennsylvania, one of my former pastors told a story that has since stuck with me. He had mentioned how he was driving back home from New York late at night, going through one of those long tunnels. Well, for one reason or another, his car broke down. Here he was in New York, late at night in the tunnel, with a broken-down vehicle. He said that he felt such a dread at that moment, knowing that he was going to have to wait for a tow truck and deal with the hassle of repairs and of getting a ride back home. During this mental self-torture, it dawned on him that at some point, he'd be at home, sitting on his comfy chair, drinking iced tea. It was only a matter of time. All he had to do was get through that passage of time, and he'd be where he wanted to be. Barring that he didn't die, it was inevitable that he would get home. So he focused on that and lo and behold, he was home after all.

I find that seeing beyond our suffering is of immense value in our fight against it. I'm in pain now, but I won't always be. You have a dim light at the end of the tunnel. But knowing that once you get through your time of suffering here on earth, you'll be in heaven with the God who saved you? That is a light with such refulgence as to blind you entirely.

But the question we must ask now is this—did I count it all joy to suffer in this way? Not exactly. But there were times when in my tearful prayers, while in this deep sorrow, I'd thank God for where I was because I knew two truths: one, that God was not going to leave me there forever, and two, that God was going to grow me through that experience and glorify Himself. What we suffer, we can share with those who suffer or who have suffered likewise. We can provide a testimony of God's goodness and love to those living apart from it, who are trying to contextualize a suffering that their worldview doesn't allow for. We can encourage our Christian brothers and sisters and share the wisdom God imparted to our aching souls, and we can glorify God for the new strength that He gives us every day to fight our battles. And sometimes, the battles we fight will continue for a lifetime. Chronic health conditions or ailments of the body that are likely not be remedied, such as losing your sight or your hearing, or an appendage—all of these things may put a person in a constant state of suffering that they must endure and trust God with. If this is where you are, do not fear, for the Lord has not forgotten you. He has not become indifferent to your sorrows. We need not look any further than the Apostle Paul who was one of the greatest apostles to have lived (according to my humble opinion). Though he was assuredly a soldier for Christ to the utmost degree, he was also one who suffered much hardship and suffering. In fact, when God calls Ananias to go and retrieve Paul after Paul's conversion to the faith (having formerly been a murderer and persecutor of the church), Ananias is fearful because of Paul's reputation. The Lord's response is this: **"Go, for he is a chosen instrument of Mine to carry My name before the Gentiles and the kings and the children of Israel. For I will show him how much he must suffer for the sake of My name"** (see Acts 9:15–16). And sure enough, Paul suffered greatly, even having a long-lasting "thorn in the flesh" that afflicted him that God refused to remove for His own purposes. Yet, Paul was deeply loved by God and served Him faithfully in the ministry he had been given, despite the sorrows he encountered through it because Paul counted all things as rubbish in comparison to the surpassing worth of Jesus Christ.

And to finish off this chapter, we return to James one last time, to finish off his exhortation that he gave to the scattered Jews facing persecution. He writes to them an encouragement that all of us would do well to etch into the very inner places of our hearts when faced with suffering. It reads, **Blessed is the man who remains steadfast under trials, for when he has stood the test he will receive the crown of life, which God has promised to those who love Him** (James 1:12).

God sees; God hears; God knows.

6

I Couldn't Find a Reason

hy am I here?
The burning question.

If there is ever an inquiry that plagues the human mind, I am confident that the question of our purpose is amongst the top of the list. All of us want to make sense of our existence in a meaningful fashion. Are we just here for a temporary, mistaken moment, or is there another reason why we walk the earth? Is there anything that marks us out as unique creatures in contrast to the crawling beasts and the slithering serpents, and if there is, what is it? Is our worth self-given or assigned by another? What is the value of our lives?

Whenever I was feeling particularly depressed, you can rest assured that these questions were not too far behind me. The purpose that I felt in one moment could just as easily vanish in the next if something that happened served to erase it. This could be something as simple as working at a high-paying job. Many of us easily find our purpose by the labor of our hands. After all, our jobs generally take a good portion of our time from us, so we might as well assign value to it. Yet, the job we so heavily invest in could be lost. The company we work for could go under, resulting in mass layoffs. We could make an egregious mistake that costs us our job. A loved one in a different state could receive a terrible diagnosis requiring us to relocate to take care of them. Or maybe the long hours have started to negatively impact our marriage and children, and we have to find something else to do. Whatever the case is, the purpose from our labor is a temporal one that can be lost just as easily as it was obtained.

For me, I found purpose in multiple facets of my life, but inevitably, those avenues of meaning would soon shut down, and when failure was thrown into the mix, then the searing pain of purposelessness erupted in my heart, and the thoughts of suicide ensued. The danger of such a formula is no secret. If I cannot justify my existence, then I can certainly justify (wrongly) in terminating it. If the trajectory of my life has gone in the opposite direction and the path seems too wayward to correct, then the overwhelming sensation of failure and lack of meaning could take me to the cliff's edge. And let's be honest—when we were all just young kids playing in the dirt, we never envisioned ourselves as growing up to be less than what we wanted for ourselves. My parents gloated that I was going to be a pastor because as a young child I was able to conceptualize truths of Scriptures. I would often preach to other kids in my class much to the chagrin of my teacher who would tell me, "M.R, I understand that you believe in the Bible, but you can't tell everyone else that they're going to hell if they don't believe in Jesus," to which I responded, "But it's true!" My parents certainly agreed, and so I ran around as an unhinged evangelist at the ripe age of eleven. Despite this, I never became a pastor. I had dreams and plans of becoming a K9 officer with a friend of mine. It never happened. I dreamed of being Prince Charming. I ended up divorced. I thought by twenty-one I'd have my life figured out. It just happened this year at the age of twenty-nine. I was going to graduate college with a bachelor's in Criminal Justice. I ended up dropping out of college. I was going to be strong and attractive. I ended up depressed, out of shape, and self-loathing. The list goes on and on. And what of the young dreamer who grows up traveling with the wrong crowd and gets into drugs, now finding themselves in a spiraling addiction? Or the girl who aspired to be a doctor who got pregnant at the age of seventeen and ends up getting an abortion, now suffocating from the guilt? She never went back to the school. Or the young man who was on fire for the Lord and went to seminary, but got embroiled in sexual affairs, pornography, and licentiousness, and ends up getting booted from seminary, now working a minimum wage job wondering if he has enough money to pay for rent?

Needless to say, none of us end up exactly where we want to end up. This can be a devastating blow to our worldview. It can denigrate our identity, the way we see ourselves, and how we perceive the world. It can jade how we view or even perceive God. More than once I have heard the common retort, "I used to believe in God, but then when x happened, I realized God couldn't possibly be real." I call this a circumstantial profession of faith. It is easy to believe in God when it seems to be that God is giving us everything we want and protecting us from everything we don't. But that kind of faith is not in God, but in convenience—the god who operates as a genie in the bottle as opposed to the sovereign Lord of the entire universe. And if the genie in the bottle isn't strong enough to keep me from stubbing my toe, then he certainly isn't worthy of my worship or adoration!

Indeed, the question of purpose is a critical one, and one we should analyze very carefully. To miss the mark on this question is to miss the mark on the entirety of the universe because as I will endeavor to show, it is all connected. And to show this, I will take you to Exhibit A, the beginning of the universe.

In all of my discussions with my atheist friends, I always go to the same place—the beginning of everything. Logically, you must do this to make sense of purpose. In my experience, arguments tend to start somewhere in the middle of the timeline. We want to discuss evidence for this or evidence for that, when in reality, such debate without a recognition of the first things is ultimately futile. This is because discussing anything without a recognition of the beginning skews the way we understand that evidence or even make sense of it. The question of everything (purpose included) can only be truly answered by understanding the beginning of everything. If there is a God, then my worldview is going to be shaped and defined by Him because He is the Creator of the universe. Theological presuppositions will be inevitable.

If there is no God, then that will shape my worldview as well. God's existence impacts every aspect of life. In a world without God, I must try to justify and define my own purpose in life in light of its temporal nature, material make-up, random occurrences, and meaninglessness. At this juncture, one may challenge me that just because God does not exist does not mean that our life is meaningless. Regarding purpose and life, Jean-Paul Sartre says in his book *Being and Nothingness*, that "life is a useless passion." Many scholars understand that if there is nothing more to this life than this life, then this life is ultimately meaningless. It comes and it goes. It starts and ends, and when it ends, it truly ends. We, as something, go down into the grave as nothings. And seeing how our life is but a vapor, and we are finite and limited and weak, then it stands to say that we truly are the embodiment of useless passions. At some point in time, all of this will end. Some cosmic event will wipe out earth as we know it; all life will be destroyed, and the chronicles of man and his history will disappear. It's this line of reasoning that an honest atheist must presume upon, for to do otherwise would be intellectually dishonest. In a godless universe, meaning is nil. All of our relativistic pursuits are nil. The value that we assign ourselves is arbitrary and fleeting. It is akin to having both feet planted firmly in midair—an exercise in futility. We have already proved it; the worth I give myself today depends on external variables. Once those variables wane, so does my perceived self-value. Ever wonder why there are so many self-help books that reinforce just how good you are, despite you knowing that's not the case? You pay someone else to tell you sweet little lies, little positive maxims to make you "feel good". Yet, these books are money grabs. The author doesn't know you. The work is impersonal and grounded in nothing objective. It is grasping at invisible straws. For example, is the blanket statement, "You're a good person who makes the world a brighter place!" applicable to the repeat sex offender? Not to their victims, it's not. But many books simply encourage their readers to be better, and so far, no harm no foul—to an extent. But what good is the pursuit of good when the end of both good men and evil men is ultimately the same? Is life only valuable when it comes with an abundance of resource or pleasures? The hedonist says so but has yet to define the purpose of himself in light of it. If purpose is subjective from person to person, then purpose is ultimately subjective, and if purpose is ultimately subjective, then purpose is ultimately worthless. If we can define our purpose, we can increase or decrease its value and this usually to our own destruction. That which can be influenced is mutable, and that which is mutable does not provide a firm foundation. At the very least, it offers no stability. But how does the existence of God provide objective meaning? Well, we first must endeavor to explore the idea of meaning. Why does anything have meaning at all? The easiest example to study in this regard are words. Words have meaning because words have been defined. That which is defined ought to operate according to categories that correlate to the reality around us and comport with the laws of the physical universe. When we define meanings of words and associate them with reality, we find structure and order. And in so far as we don't begin to twist those words' meanings like a wax nose, we have consistency. To disparage meaning and definitions is to assault reality itself. When we strip words of their meanings, we can no longer identify them or provide them purpose. The question of purpose then touches on the question of identity.

IDENTITY

When a person with gender dysphoria expresses their dysphoria, how do they do it? By making the claim, "I identify as…" This declaration is an announcement as much as it is a request: "I identify as *x*; therefore, I want all of you to refer to me as *x*." At the very least, the request is, "Respect my *xness*." What is really being sought after is validation—the validation of existence by confirming my self-perception as it pertains to my esteemed worth.

Everybody has an identity. Most people give themselves their identities. They find a group that matches the characteristics or ideals that they share and then subsume themselves under that umbrella. Because of this, most people tend to conform themselves to the ideals of that identity, as to cement their identity further into it. Identities can be polarizing if the identities are naturally conflicting. Democrats and Republicans are vastly different from one another, so much so that they have their own respective parties. Catholics are Catholics, and Christians are not Muslims. These distinct groups allow us to separate ourselves in ways that we feel are significant, that touch on the very essence of who we are. Now, if our identity provides us our purpose, or our association with a certain tribe offers us creature comforts by way of validation, then what would it mean for someone to come in and disagree with our beliefs and identity? In reality, it would mean that individuals are individuals who have individualistic opinions about different topics and beliefs; it means that there is diversity within humanity. Yet, we see more often than not that if person A voices an opinion different from person B, that person B goes on the offensive and begins to utter a whole slew of derogatory remarks toward person A. Why? Because in today's world, the minds of individuals have been taught what to think and not how to think. They've been taught to view a dissenting view as an attack because if you tell me that my identity is wrong, you're saying that my purpose is wrong, and an attack on what I identify with is a direct attack on me and those like me.

Those who espouse such a defense mechanism denigrate their own value and self-worth—they have a shallow outlook on just how valuable they are because to contribute the entirety of your worth to a group identity is to say that you have nothing intrinsically valuable to offer as an individual outside of that collective. You lose you by entering the hive mindset. You become like everyone else in your clique, and thus, you're more lost than before you entered it—the tree lost amidst the forest. No better example can be given of this than an interview that Jordan Peterson had with Helen Lewis. At one point in the interview, Jordan Peterson remarked,

> "I'm not hearing what you think, I'm hearing, what, how
> you're able to represent the ideology you were taught. And
> it's not that interesting because I don't know anything about
> you. I could replace you with someone else who thinks the
> same way and that means you're not here. That's what it
> means. It's not pleasant. So you're not, you're not drawing,
> you're not integrating the specifics of your personal experience

*with what you've been taught—to synthesize something
that's genuine and surprising and engaging in a narrative
sense as a consequence, and that's the pathology of ideological
possession. It's not good. And it's not good that I, that I know
where you stand on things once I know a few things, it's like,
why have a conversation? I already know where you stand
on things."*

I remember hashing this out with a gentleman I once worked with. He told me about a bad experience he had in church because nobody in the church would affirm his homosexuality, and thus he felt attacked. This prompted him to leave the church altogether due to feeling like he could never belong.

Up until that point, I had not discussed with him my faith or my views of homosexuality, so I figured this would be a good time to explore his life and experiences. When he shared his church history with me, I asked him if he felt like I had hated him or been antagonistic toward him. He looked genuinely shocked and said, "No!" I told him that I was a Christian and didn't affirm homosexuality. I asked him if he had felt like I had treated him as lesser than any of our other coworkers. Again, he said no. I explained to him that maybe the issue wasn't that the church didn't affirm his identity; maybe the issue was his perception of what that meant. He took it to mean that the church dismissed him as a person because they wouldn't affirm his main identity as a good thing. He took it as an attack, despite the fact that no one there demeaned him for it. You may say in response, "But to not affirm is to demean!" but this couldn't be further from the truth. Many I know do not affirm my Christian faith, but that doesn't mean that they have demeaned me at all. And even if they did, it wouldn't make a difference to me because I know how God defines me.

Despite how strong your adherence is to your identity now, that does not mean that it cannot change later. New information, new experiences, and new developments can easily change what you most strongly identify with, if your identity is left in your own hands to determine. So even this, as grounded as it may seem, is also temporal and fleeting, and thus we're brought back to God.

If God is, then that means that God created the entire material universe. That means that He has defined it, and because God is perfect, His definitions are also perfect. If He has defined it, then He has given everything meaning objectively, including suffering. Thus, when we operate as agents in this world, we operate according to God's defined reality. Men are men and women are women because God has decreed it to be. Truth is because God is, and it is Jesus who says, **"I am the way, and the truth, and the life"** (see John 14:6; emphasis mine). You can suppress the truth of reality, but you cannot destroy it. To do so would require you to be greater than God, and if you were that, then you would be God!

If God is, then God is the one who has created not only me, but the entirety of mankind. He who creates, defines. So as it were, God created us, and God defined us. We were created in His image (Genesis 1:26–27), made for the express purpose of worshiping Him (Psalm 86:9; Isaiah 60:21; Romans 11:36; 1 Corinthians 6:20, 10:31; Revelation 4:11) and enjoying Him forever (Psalm 16:5–11, 144:15; Isaiah 12:2; Luke 2:10; Philippians 4:4; Revelation 21:3–4). In this, I obtain value and purpose according to the One who has fashioned me by His power. Not only me, but every single person on this earth! That is why every person deserves dignity, value, and respect. Not because we are inherently worthy, but because we have been made and defined by Him who is inherently worthy.

If my purpose and value (and my identity) are assigned by God, then no power on heaven or earth can remove them from me. No dissent can diminish who God says that I am in Christ. I have an identity that is unshakable, immovable, impregnable. I have a guarantee that does not grow or diminish because it is perfect. What God declares no man can foist. He is absolutely sovereign over all things (Psalm 2:1–4).

What this means is that no matter what your lot is in life, you have an objective purpose. Your life matters objectively in the most meaningful of ways. You were created for a reason. You were created in God's image, made for His glory. Whether your life aligns with that maxim, I cannot know, but despite this, I can still encourage you to reevaluate yourself in light of God's Word—in light of the truth of His revelation. Can you be anything other than what God has declared you to be?

Going back to my atheistic friends, their worldview can be summarized as follows: the origin of the universe is unknown, but we can know that the universe as we perceive came to be through a cosmic event called the Big Bang. Eventually, non-life became life on earth, and creatures began to form through millions of series of micro and macro adaptations. The single cell eventually became a fish, and a fish eventually became a philosopher. Everything that occurred had no guiding force, no Creator, no defining. It just was. And now, we are here until we're not. If my friends are correct, then I'd have to wonder if we're simply the byproducts of chemical reactions in the brains. I'd have to wonder if we matter at all, or if anything matters in the final analysis.

I have often heard it said that our being here was simply a mistake or an accident. But this misses the mark because making a mistake or having an accident requires a person to make them. It requires (1) a mind, and (2) an intention. If the universe is a mistake, what was the intention, and whose intention was it? Furthermore, why hasn't it been corrected? If it was a mistake, how could we even know unless that information was revealed to us?

Essentially, the atheist leaves his world open, undetermined, and unknowable, but at the same time, lives his life as if that were not the case. The relative ease in which an atheist simply says, "I don't know the origin and I don't care," is astounding. The most fundamental, existential question is the one most often overlooked or swept under the rug. I have yet to hear a compelling origin account that does not violate the laws of logic. If there is no God, we live in an indifferent universe where the categories of good and evil simply cease to be because they cannot be defined objectively. What is good today could be evil tomorrow depending on who is in the driver's seat. What you find purposeful today could be declared tomorrow as immoral. There're no rules to play by except the ones made up on the fly. Is this truly representative of the human experience? I don't think so.

Plagued by the problem of purpose is Solomon, the wisest man in the Bible. He records his toils of finding purpose outside of God in the book of Ecclesiastes, seeking meaning in all the things that man could desire: work, money, relationships, and invention. Listen to his words:

> *Vanity of vanities, says the Preacher, vanity of vanities! All is vanity. What does man gain by all the toil at which he toils under the sun? A generation goes, and a generation comes, but the earth remains forever.… All things are full of weariness; a man cannot utter it; the eye is not satisfied with seeing, nor the ear filled with hearing. What has been is what will be, and what has been done is what will be done, and there is nothing new under the sun.* (1:2–4, 8–9)

The thesis statement of Solomon is that all is vanity, or purposeless. We come, we go, but the earth remains. The changing variable is us. Nothing can truly satisfy our inner cravings, the appetite of our souls (see Ecclesiastes 3:11). How did Solomon draw this conclusion? We keep in mind that Solomon was king. He was rich, powerful, and had all the wisdom he could ask for.[43] Despite this, he still had to endeavor to learn from where man draws purpose. He first tries with wisdom (1:12–18) but concludes, **For in much wisdom is much vexation, and he who increases in knowledge increases sorrow. He tries to indulge himself in multiple pleasures: I said in my heart, "Come now, I will test you with pleasure; enjoy yourself." But behold, this also was vanity. I said of laughter, "It is mad," and of pleasure, "What use is it?"** (2:1–2).

And I suppose that's the true question—what use is pleasure? Especially in light of the fact that pleasures are always temporal and fleeting. They do not truly satisfy. Yet, the common response of those who struggle with finding purpose or having a meaningful existence tend to gravitate toward seeking out vain pleasures as a means of passing time by to escape their existential crisis. The lonely person who wants validation from a partner but cannot find one turns toward pornography in hopes of finding something there that can replicate the satiation of having a significant other. Pleasurable? Carnally, you bet. Fulfilling?

---

[43] See 2nd Chronicles 2:7–12.

Not a chance. We're like the woman at the well in John 4 who drinks water only to thirst again, when Christ offers us eternal life through living waters (see John 4:1–26). Like Israel in the desert wilderness, we yearn for manna from heaven to fill our stomachs for a moment only to grumble the next hour when we're hungry. But those pleasures never elicit gratitude, only expectations. I can't imagine that a man, before closing his laptop after consuming licentiousness, says, "Why, thank you very much, friends! I really appreciate the show you put on for me. Means a lot." More than likely, he closes the laptop and moves on to the next thing. It could be Netflix, video games, or some other hobby. Maybe he goes to bed (hopefully after taking a shower). But the thrill is gone, the pleasure vanishes, and the gaping truth of a meaningless existence is ever before him—and don't you dare think it's not there just because he looks away from it. We aren't the little kids anymore who pull their covers over their faces at everything that goes bump in the night. To be sure, the claw and fangs of a true monster spares no sheet or blanket—no matter the thread count. The action of ignoring the truth or acting as if it is not, then, is the action of suppressing or stifling. We push down as hard as we can, smothering its effect on our conscience. We have to do this—the outlook of a godless universe is too grim to bear.

So laughter and pleasure are knocked out of the game. Who else is playing?

I searched with my heart how to cheer my body with wine—my heart still guiding me with wisdom—and how to lay hold of folly, till I might see what was good for the children of man to do under heaven during the few days of their life (Ecclesiastes 2:3–4). The quest for purpose continues, this time with the comfort of wine. Alcohol is a go-to for many in the world for its ability to numb our conscience and take us away from the problems of today. But herein lies the folly— alcohol does not remove our problems. When we ignore our problems by consumption of alcohol, our problems continue to pile up. Interestingly enough, Solomon is seeking this question out, not only for himself, but for the "children of man." In other words, the children of man hadn't found the answer to the problem of purpose either. Like Solomon, the world was searching and coming up empty-handed. This makes sense, of course. If the wisest man on the earth cannot discover the answer, then could we truly expect anyone else to discover it before him? Certainly not! And Solomon doesn't mince words here—man truly lives a breath before perishing, but despite this, his value and purpose have not been stolen from him. He still matters.

The next portion of Solomon's writing contains an account of his many magnificent works and creations (vv. 4–6), his exorbitant wealth and purchasing power (vv. 7–8), his surpassing worth of all persons in the land (v. 9), and his absolute indulgence in all pleasures without restraint (v. 10). Don't miss this. Solomon had everything he could want in this world. He was the upper echelon whose hand knew no restraint. If Solomon wanted women, he had them. If he wanted grand architecture and monuments, they were completed. Any pleasure available, Solomon took hold of for himself. Money was an endless resource, but **He who loves money will not be satisfied with money, nor he who loves wealth with his income; this also is vanity** (5:10). No matter what man has, it will never satisfy.

"But Solomon didn't have all the modern luxuries we have now!" This is true, albeit, irrelevant. Solomon could have lived in 2022. Do you think his conclusions would have been any different? Are there any pleasures in today's world that would eclipse the pleasures of Solomon as king over Israel? Surely not, for even today, we hear of the elite committing suicide, being caught up in scandals, and suffering depression and addiction. That is the result of having everything in the world except purpose—it's not good. Material goods cannot grant us purpose, neither can pleasures. As Solomon says, **Better is a little with the fear of the LORD than great treasure and trouble with it** (Proverbs 15:16).

So what was Solomon's response after he had pursued all of these other avenues of finding purpose? **Then I considered all that my hands had done and the toil I had expended in doing it, and behold, all was vanity and a striving after wind, and there was nothing to be gained under the sun** (2:11). Truly, no matter what we gain, there is always something we are losing—time—and with it, our lives. Every second of the clock is one tick closer to your demise. You are coming to the end of yourself, my friend, and you aren't aware of it. Or maybe you are, and it eats you alive. "Well, I'm young and healthy," you reason. And I grant you this. But the drunk driver whose blood alcohol is twice the legal limit whose large truck crushes your small sedan isn't. And now neither are you. Jesus illustrates this principle well in a parable that He tells in Luke 12. We read,

> And [Jesus] told them a parable, saying, "The land of a rich man produced plentifully, and he thought to himself, 'What shall I do, for I have nowhere to store my crops?' And he said, 'I will do this: I will tear down my barns and build larger ones, and there I will store all my grain and my goods. And I will say to my soul, "Soul, you have ample goods laid up for many years; relax, eat, drink, be merry."' But God said to him, "'Fool! This night your soul is required of you, and the things you have prepared, whose will they be?'" So is the one who lays up treasure for himself and is not rich toward God." (vv. 16–21)

You'll recall we reviewed this very same passage to warn against basing your life on your possessions in chapter three. Yet, the wisdom of God spreads itself over many scenarios. Solomon and Jesus are saying the same thing: what good are the things of this life only if they miss the life that comes after? And this life isn't a guarantee—you're living on borrowed time. You may be thinking, "If life is so vain, why do anything at all? Why not just sit, watch the wall, and wait to die?" So far, it has not been rainbows and sunshine. But the truth is, the things that Solomon tried to enjoy or find purpose in failed him because God was not in the equation. But when Solomon put God as his top priority, then he found enjoyment from all the good things that God gave him because those things are enjoyed in light of God, not in spite of Him. Life is only vain when you attempt to live it apart from your Creator: **This is the end of the matter; all has been heard. Fear God and keep His commandments, for this is the whole duty**

of man. For God will bring every deed into judgment, with every secret thing, whether good or evil (Ecclesiastes 12:13–14).

THE PROBLEM OF EVIL

There's another side to the question of purpose: what is the purpose of evil and suffering? What is the purpose of depression, of death, of things sinister and foul? This question is used as an argument against God. If God is all good, then how could He allow evil to exist? It's the paradox that Lex Luthor presents to Superman: "If God is all-powerful, then He cannot be all good, and if God is all good, then He cannot be all powerful."

However, there are a few philosophical conundrums with this question. It assumes that God must immediately eradicate all evil. Well, He certainly can, but that does not bode well for us as sinners, does it? What evil is perpetrated on this earth? The evil schemes of men. To ask God to rid the world of evil is to ask Him for Noah's flood, except this time, without saving anyone. Cats and dogs don't rob convenience stores. Horned owls aren't pushing drugs on street corners, and Kangaroos aren't involved in illegal, underground fighting rings (although they'd probably do pretty well). Man is the source of evil because it was man who disobeyed God in the garden. We stipulate that God must do something and therefore because He hasn't, we assert that God cannot possibly exist. But who's in charge? sovereign God or temporal man? Who sets the rules? And who decides ultimately how evil is handled? God.

But the problem of evil doesn't go away by dismissing God—it grows exponentially worse. You cannot know what is evil unless you know what is good. In a godless world, who's to say? You can subjectively assert an ethic, but you cannot universally bind it. In this system, it is the strong who decides what is good and what is evil. It's Nazi Germany dehumanizing Jews and saying it is good to exterminate them. It is slave owners in America calling Africans property and beating them bloody. It is radical feminists marching down Washington demanding the right to murder their babies. Do you see how the battle of good and evil, if left in the hands of man, will always come to blows? Power rules, but power also corrupts. A subjective ethic is no ethic at all—it is tyranny and submission. So nothing is truly good or evil, which means crimes cannot objectively exist. Man has no inherent value. Kicking a rock and kicking a human makes no difference. In all actuality, based on a godless worldview, the rock should be more esteemed, for it far outlasts the temporal body of man. The reality is—and this is nothing new—that evil presupposes good, and good presupposes God, because again, you cannot have good without an appeal to a standard, and that standard is the character of God Himself. Don't agree? There's one relatively known atheist who would certainly agree with this assessment. His name is Richard Dawkins.[44]

But even in his astute assessment, Dawkins appeals to words such as selfish, lucky, reason, and justice in a world where those things cannot objectively exist outside of God. One thing he does get right, however, is that in a godless universe, you cannot rationally have moral qualms. Pitiless indifference is all that remains. So what we are saying here is that in order to indict God for the problem of evil, God has to first *be*, or else there's no way to indict Him to begin with. There's no standard. But attempting to indict God by God is a fool's errand. It cannot be done. The Judge of all the Earth is judged by no one.

The other assumption regarding Lex Luthor's statement is that if God does not deal with evil on the horizontal plane, then that means it will never be dealt with. But the truth is, all of us will be judged for our evil and rebellion. We will all have to provide an account. For some, we will be found covered by the righteousness of Christ who took our sins from us through His atonement, paid them in full, and credited us His right standing with God. For others, they will be found only in their sins, and God will judge them to hell. All evil will be dealt with in the most meaningful way—it will stand before the Lord.

---

[44] Dawkins says, "In a universe of electrons and selfish genes, blind physical forces and genetic replication, some people are going to get hurt, other people are going to get lucky, and you won't find any rhyme or reason in it, nor any justice. The universe that we observe has precisely the properties we should expect if there is, at bottom, no design, no purpose, no evil, no good, nothing but pitiless indifference."

What we need to recognize then is that while evil is a lack of the good (which is a lack of God's righteousness), it does not exist as a force itself, as if it were a battle between God and Satan. In the same way that darkness has no substance, neither does evil. When the light is turned on, darkness is expelled. It cannot resist it. When the good is "turned on", so to speak, evil disappears. So God, being all good, can use the evils of men for His greater good and purpose (see Genesis 50:20; Acts 2:23–24). In fact, God actively restrains the evil of men as a common grace (Romans 1:24, 26, 28). We are not as evil as we could be.

So then, what purpose does our suffering and depression serve? For starters, it is a reminder that our strength and life come not from ourselves, but from God (Acts 17:28). The weakness of man is always meant to drive us toward God who we often neglect in times of health and prosperity. It also reminds us of how sinister sin is, and the ill-effects of the Fall. This calls us to worship God for His provisions and redemption found in Christ, who He did not have to send to save us but chose to as an act of grace.

We also bear in mind that God is sovereign over all things, which means that the purpose of our suffering is in His hands. We may not understand it. It may grow wearisome as suffering often does, but it is controlled. Now, this is not to absolve anyone of their own responsibility or contribution to their own suffering. God is not sitting up in heaven throwing lightning bolts down upon innocent man like a juvenile trickster. Our woes result from our sin nature collectively. Another person is rude, inflammatory, and derogatory toward me. This in turn angers me or saddens me. Another person manifested sin toward me, and because the consequences of sin is death and destruction, it is no surprise that there was some kind of negative effect on me by experiencing that phenomenon. But then there are things that I do that contribute to my misery. I engage in a particular sin that bathes me in guilt and self-condemnation, I tell a white lie at work for the third time and get fired; I speed through a red light and get a ticket; we are more often than not our own greatest enemies. Despite this, God's grace abounds for us all. Jesus says, "**[God] makes His sun rise on the evil and on the good, and sends rain on the just and the unjust**" (see

Matthew 5:45). God allows us to enjoy the beauty and splendor of this life. He gives us every breath. That doesn't mean that every breath is pleasant or that every experience is dynamic and prosperous for us at the moment, but what it does mean is that God is over all things, even to the point of calling the sun His own possession. In God, everything has a purpose according to His will, and because God is all good and all knowing, everything He does is the best thing that can be done. We may not agree in our suffering, but the Lord's thoughts and ways are not our own—they're higher and greater (Isaiah 55:8). We cannot probe into the secret counsel of God unless it has been explicitly revealed in His Word to us, and thankfully God does communicate to us that He is Lord over all creation. Even the problem of evil is not beyond His sovereignty, but rather, is subsumed by it and used to display His justice and grace in the cross of Christ.

But before we close out this chapter, I want to reiterate your purpose, beloved. You are not a mistake. You are not an accident. You are not worthless, not unloved, not overlooked, not common, not meaningless— as long as breath embodies your lungs, you are not without hope. You were made in the image of God, and no one can take that from you.

I remember a time back when my life seemed to be a downward spiral. My (first) marriage was crumbling, I was at odds with my family, and I was working two dead-end jobs. I remember sitting on the floor, broken, destitute and ashamed, feeling hopeless. Alone. Lost. I sat in tears, feeling the desire to take myself out of this world. I didn't see a light at the end of the tunnel, yet I still had the Lord with me. Though I did not deserve Him, I had a God who loved me, who cared for me, and who was there for me. A God who looked upon my suffering and knew (see Exodus 2:23–25). And in this time of sorrow, I remember praying, "God, I feel like a loser, and like I don't matter. I haven't done anything right and feel like I shouldn't be here, but that doesn't matter because I know who You say that I am. Thank You for not leaving me."

Christ was my hope, my anchor within the soul. In Jesus, though the world beset me, I am safe. In Jesus, though I suffer, I am secure. Through Jesus I know who I am, what my purpose is, and to whom I belong. I know that what comes next will be so entirely glorious that to ever spend a waking moment thinking about the miseries of this life would be impossible. So will you live in light of God's truth, or will you remain in the dark?

The remaining question we have to ask then is how can we use our God given purpose to glorify Him? Well, to start, you have to know Him. Spend time in His Word and prayer. The next thing I would say is that you have a unique circle of people around you. You're in a unique place that I am not. You have skills, talents, and abilities that others do not. So you think about how to use those things to build the kingdom of God. For me, it's writing books and trying to get them into the hands of others who need them. A lot of the times, I buy my own books just to hand them out. A soul is worth more than a penny. But I also write because this way, I leave something behind to continue to work for God when I'm gone. How much has God's people and the world benefited from the works of their brothers and sisters in Christ who left something behind for them? I'd be lost without my collection of R.C. Sproul and Charles Spurgeon books!

The other aspect of finding purpose is being content with where God has you in the now. It doesn't mean do not strive to be better. Work hard. Be diligent. Take accountability and make no excuses for yourself. And surround yourself with others who want the best for you and who have their minds oriented to the same purpose of living for Christ that you do. **So, whether you eat or drink, or whatever you do, do all to the glory of God** (1 Corinthians 10:31). All the work of your hands, do it to the glory of God. How you raise your children, do it to the glory of God. How you love your wife, mow your lawn, interact with your bank teller, or walk your dog, do likewise. Do not try to find your purpose in vanity and do not let this world define you—only God has the power and right to do so. And do not despise yourself for where you are in life in comparison to others. Trust that God can use you exactly where He has you, and whether you're the CEO of some company or a tent maker like Paul (Acts 18:1–4), work as unto the Lord and never forget what He says about you: you have purpose.

7

Nor See its Hidden Worth

I have never heard of a person asking God, "Why me, Lord?" when they receive the promotion they've always wanted at work or when they're able to snatch that television deal on Black Friday. I've never seen a person proclaim, "My life is good—therefore, God is not real," nor have I ever witnessed a person angrily shaking their fist at God when they receive a good medical diagnosis.

When we flip the script, however, it's a different story. Then God is the tyrant. Then God is the monster, the divine trickster casting down lightning bolts from His chariot over top of humanity. We curse and question God in our sufferings, but we never stop to do the same when things go well. If we're being honest, perhaps we can admit that when things go well, we tend to neglect God until we need Him again (despite the fact that we always need Him). This is easiest to see in the narrative of the Judges. When Israel was being conquered after practicing wickedness and having God withdraw His blessing and favor, the people of Israel cried out to God for relief. In His mercy and compassion, God would send a judge who would help Israel find relief from their plight. When God was rescuing Israel, then Israel was God's number one fan. When the matter was resolved, however, then God became obsolete in the eyes of His people. They went back to their sinful and wicked ways. Consistent sin and rebellion manifested itself in idolatry:

> *And there arose another generation after them who did not know the LORD or the work that He had done for Israel. And the people of Israel did what was evil in the sight of the LORD and served the Baals. And they abandoned the LORD, the God of their fathers, who had brought them out of the land of Egypt. They went after other gods, from the among the gods of the peoples who were around them, and they bowed to them. And they provoked the LORD to anger.* (Judges 2:10b–12)

This cycle of forsaking the Lord repeated ad nauseam. Israel was faithless and chased after other gods. To worship other gods rather than the one true God is nothing new. We do the same in today's world by worshiping fame, power, money, and self. Anything that takes the place of God in our hearts is an idol, which means they are vast and plenty if we are not carefully examining ourselves.

Why did the people go after foreign gods? The prior generation was not teaching and instilling the mercies that God had demonstrated to them by freeing them from the bondage and cruelty of Egypt. They did know the Lord. We tend to leave behind or neglect the things that we do not value. When Israel strayed from God, it was because they did not value Him or esteem Him as the God who rescued them from the snares of Egypt. They forgot the faithfulness of the Lord, chasing after idols because those idols were more palatable to swallow. You had goddesses of fertility, gods of life and vegetation, gods of war, and a whole other host of deities who served the people in their desire for carnal pleasures. Many of the pagan gods and goddesses worship indulged the sin nature of the person. Orgies and lewd sexual practices were not uncommon. Profane sacrifices of children were also practiced, "securing" the blessing of the gods. Perhaps the people of Israel thought that God was too restrictive or too holy for their preference. The gods of the pagans looked far more enticing. Perhaps the Israelites felt that God wasn't giving them enough to satisfy their carnal pleasures. Whatever the case, the people chased what they valued, despite what they chased not being real.

When we experience suffering, we tend to view suffering as something with no value, no purpose. We don't like it and it doesn't feel good. And if it doesn't feel good, we reason, then that means that it isn't good. It is no surprise then that when people undergo suffering, they simply want to find the quickest route away from it. When the suffering is deep, such as depression, our attempts to escape it becomes all the more radical. If I struggle with memories of childhood trauma that affect me in the here and now, I may be tempted to go to alcohol or drugs or lewd behavior as a means of escapism. I may recognize that in the long run, these things will hurt me. But in the immediate sense, I obtain relief—relief from something so burdensome that it really does feel like pleasure at the moment. So I trade my future health to alleviate my current pain. This is sacrifice in reverse. Generally speaking, the idea of sacrifice is to give something up now to secure or preserve something in the future. It was for this reason why pagan nations would practice child sacrifice. "If I offer my child up to Moloch on this altar, then Moloch will surely bless me in the future."

The same principle can be seen in matters of everyday life. I sacrifice time five days of the week to go to the gym so that I can secure a healthier me for the future. I put money aside into investments (immediate loss of resource) to grow that money for the future. Sacrifice in this sense is economically motivated. But when we sacrifice the future for now, we're working backwards. Eventually, that future and the present will collide. I drink every day to clear my mind of pain. Every day, I'm hurting my liver. I'm gaining unhealthy weight. I'm slowly killing myself and my brain. But I'm avoiding dealing with the mental trauma of my life, that is, until my drinking nearly kills me. If I'm wise, then the drinking stops. Then I have to live away from my dependence from alcohol and deal with the symptoms of my trauma that I've suppressed all of those years prior. I didn't mean any harm—I just wanted to get rid of the trauma and the suffering. It had no value.

But what if we could change the way that we looked at the problem of suffering and depression? What if we saw it as a blessing? As something that God chose specifically for us for His own purposes and our own good? This certainly does not mean that we should not try to take care of our depression or our sufferings. Surely if I break my leg, I should not feel inclined to crawl down the street howling in pain, "This is the lot that God chose for me and I'm going to glorify Him now!" I, being a responsible adult, should take care of the body that God has entrusted to me. We make the distinction then that depression and suffering are not inherently good things. They are the result of the Fall. But they are also not inherently good things in the hands of an ultimately good God. And if we view our ailments through this lens, then we can come away knowing that our sufferings have a utility to them. This viewpoint removes us as victims. When I view my depression, for example, as something that God has endowed to me according to His will, then I can take courage knowing that the God who chose me for this has a plan for it. I may not know the reason, but I can trust it, nonetheless. So what are some benefits that we can glean from depression and suffering? Firstly, my testimony can be shared to the encouragement and strengthening of others. It can also share awareness to those who may be unfamiliar with depression, and it allows me to relate to those who share my experiences. And as mentioned elsewhere, this book is a result of my depression. Because I have suffered depression, I know just how terrible of a struggle it can be, and I want to help people find hope and solace in Christ wherein I found the strength to overcome. To take it further, what kick started this book was the unexpected death of my Bible mentor, Ken. I only wish he were here to see it now! Secondly, our suffering is a reminder of our frailty and our dependence. What spurred Israel's disobedience was life without trial—when things became good enough without God. When did Israel desire God and repent? When they tasted the fruit of a life without His provision and blessing—when they felt His anger and the oppression of the pagan nations. It has always been in my brokenness where I feel God's warmth the most—when I am on my knees in tears. There is something about being able to go before God in such a state and know that He cares about you and that He's listening intently. It's also another powerful truth to bear in mind that Christ is interceding for me to the Father as my Mediator (1 Timothy 2:5–6) and that even when I don't have the words to express myself in prayer, God's Spirit understands me (Romans 8:26).

Just recently the other night, I had gotten into a silly disagreement with my wife. I was already frustrated with some other things prior to the disagreement, and so I found myself becoming angrier and angrier. I went to go pray, and my prayer was anything but sophisticated or elegant. It was a maelstrom of emotions and venting frustrations. At some points, I found myself repeating my words, not sure if I was truly making sense. I didn't have to, though, because God knew what was in my heart and what I was trying to say. So even when you do not feel like prayer will make a difference, trust that it will because it does. It does not mean that God will grant every petition but spending time alone with God to pray is an indispensable tool that Christians tend to overlook in the dealings of their busy lives. We should never be too busy for our Lord.

Thirdly, depression gives Christians a strong witness in the world by reflecting the joy of Christ in their lives despite their sufferings. In fact, some of the strongest preachers I love have battled with depression in some form or another, with Charles Spurgeon at the top of the list. Some other notable theologians were Augustine, Jonathan Edwards, John Wesley, Søren Kierkegaard, and Martin Luther. All of these men were titans of the faith, and the church would suffer great loss indeed without their contributions. Each of these men battled with bouts of depression, but they trusted in God and overcame it, the same way that you and I can. When people look in on us as believers and see that we have joy amidst suffering because of Christ, it may open up the conversation to the gospel and lead a soul to the Lord. Recall that man is made with eternity in his heart (Ecclesiastes 3:11), which means mankind is searching for the peace that only God can give. However, because of their sin nature, they want the benefits of God without the rule of God. They want heaven—they just don't want God to be there when they arrive. When you have answers to their problem and can articulate Christ, the Spirit of God may work through your sharing for the salvation of their souls. That is something to think about!

Fourthly, our suffering, if rightly understood, draws us closer to God in gratitude. We can praise God for His provisions and His strength, praise Him for His wisdom in what He has given unto us, and glorify Him when we finally understand why He gave us a burden to begin with. Some may contest this and say it would be better if no suffering existed at all, but suffering is not something God handed down to us. It is not something He created to punish us with. Suffering comes through sin and is rightfully deserved. The world lives in constant rebellion and animosity toward their Creator, yet rail against Him for not "doing enough" for them at the same time. That is quite an arrogant accusation. To be sure, God is a holy and righteous judge. He is obligated by His nature and character to judge sin, but He is not required to show mercy to sinners. When God uses our suffering to our benefit and His glory, He is being gracious to us. We do not have to rejoice in the pain itself, but we can rejoice in the good that comes out of it if we so choose to trust God's providence.

A few years ago, when I first moved to Yuma, I was talking with my brother as we were in line for Starbucks. I told him that I was thankful for what God had taught me through my prior marriage. I did not see the divorce or the fallout as a good thing and there was much sin involved, but I praised God that He redeemed that situation by helping me grow as a man. It was my prior divorce that spurned me to write a book on relationships called *Fractured Together*, the very same book, coincidentally, that convinced my wife to marry me! And my time in Phoenix where I dealt with radical guilt and depression rallied me to write the book *Peter on Saturday: and the Problem of Guilt*. This book has helped those who have read it have a better understanding on how God deals with our guilt, and how we can have a clear conscience in Christ, despite our sullied pasts. The power of how our suffering can be used for good truly does depend on how much we trust God with it. That doesn't mean we cannot pray for it to go away or that we go looking for trouble. But what it does mean is that when we come across the inevitable roadblocks of life, that we are equipped and prepared to deal with them.

Lastly, depression and suffering have a way of driving the mind to more intellectual pursuits. As I became more familiar with the condition of my depression, I developed curiosities about how its existence could coincide with my faith—and on a grander scale—how evil could seem to coexist with good on earth. I was driven to the Bible to comb through its pages, seek after wisdom, and push for more knowledge. I dug through the commentaries and sermons of faithful preachers and men of God. The more that I learned, the more grounded I became in my faith, and now the things that I have learned, I share with you in the hopes of encouraging you in your fight and your battle against depression.

There are many other reasons that others could come up with to show how a good God can use the evil and sufferings of this world to His glory and our benefit. Though the experiences we face on this earth are truly grand, they do not by any means have to define our existence or strip us of the joys of life. When God can take something as gruesome as the cross and use it as an instrument to display both His justice and mercy to reconcile sinners to Himself, then we ought to be sure that He can use our depression too.

8

So I Went to Close
the Curtain

S *uicide.*

I hate this word with a deep agony. When I see the word, hear the word, or think of the word, my eyes often well up. When I read others' accounts of how a loved one's suicide impacted them or read the accounts of those who have taken their own lives, I mourn inside. It's painful to consider. I hate the idea of someone coming to the end of themselves in such a way as to feel that their only option left is to put an end to their life. I often wish I had but just a few fleeting moments with them in such a dark hour, to plead with them, to tell them that everything is okay and that they aren't alone—that there is hope.

But alas, such is not my lot in life, nor theirs. But the pain remains all the same. Sometimes, I find myself contemplating at random times of the day the stark and cold reality of suicide, its growing rates in the United States, and how this problem has even invaded the lives of our youth to an alarming degree—how it seems to have become the go-to option for the downtrodden in spirit.

Perhaps I hate the word suicide, in part, because it has shaped the cursed landscape of a hurting mind—my own. What I suffered with for a great majority of my life was suicidal depression. Even writing it on paper makes my eyes hot. It has such a weight to it, suicide, that can reasonably feel overbearing. But where does this malady—this emotional torrent of hell—come from? Why do we experience this and why do we at times desire it?

In one sense, I am not entirely vocal about my depression, but in another sense, I make no qualms to share the nature of it to those who ask or when the situation calls for it. I've even shared with others rather openly that I suffered from suicidal tendencies. Many are surprised, or perhaps uncomfortable, at such a revelation. Others quietly acquiesce to what they were just told. Some respond with something like, "Yeah, I've had suicidal thoughts before, too." If only it was that simple!

A sparing thought of suicide is common. Many of us, embroiled in emotional tycoons have had the thought in passing, "It'd be so much easier if I wasn't here!" Bills, relational problems, self-image issues—the laundry list continues. But that is a fraction of time. For others, like myself, the vein of suicide lies much deeper in the skin and bleeds much heavier when pricked. It's not a fleeting thought, but a continuous one in your mind constantly, attacking unexpectedly when you thought you were experiencing a brief reprieve. It especially manifests itself in any form of pain, suffering, or grief. For some, suicide is a response to a problem for which the answer seems impossible to grab hold of. For others, it's the end of a suffering that was seemingly immortal. Then there are those who feel they have no place in the world but the grave, and maybe not even there, because what good is a grave if no one will come to visit you—if no one will shed a tear at your departure? Or perhaps it's the definitive resolution to an existential crisis of a meaningless existence in an indifferent world. Maybe still, it's one fleeting and final attempt to find solidarity with a cruel world by abandoning yourself like everyone else has, or the ticket out of this life after committing a gross injustice, such as a mass shooting. Whatever the reason—a cheating spouse, the loss of a child, loss of a job, crippling and merciless guilt, post-traumatic stress disorder after serving one's country—the problem of suicide is real, and it isn't going anywhere.

This is one of those monsters that doesn't sleep under your bed. No, this is the sort that opens its jaws, crowns your skull with jagged teeth, and dares you to fight back. It is, in my estimation, Satan's favorite device.

My problem with suicidal depression started at age fourteen and has been with me ever since, eating away at me moment by moment. At many intervals in my life, I've almost lost it all in the battle, almost lost hope, almost grabbed the pills, almost grabbed the knife, gazed upon a loaded gun from across the room, contemplatively. My mind has wandered to and fro, sometimes hand-in-hand with depression, at other times abusively dragged by suicide. I know what it is to stare at the ceiling at night estimating how much fight I had left—if I'd make it to the end of the week or if this was the finale of an exhaustive struggle. I know how it feels to lock eyes with my niece, barely old enough to utter a word, and wonder if she'd grow up without me. Long and lonely drives, staring out the window, hands on the wheel knowing that they were in control of a 2,000-pound machine much more fortuitous than the body driving it. I've wrestled with selfishness, imagined the funeral, writing the note, others reading it, how it may hurt for a time, but life would go on because what other choice does it have? I know what it's like to feel like God has abandoned you in your darkest hour. I've been there, on my knees, crying aloud for God to grant me the strength not to kill myself. What a prayer.

All of this to say, suicide is not something I write about from the outside looking in. It is a very vivid reality for me and if you struggle with it, then I know it is for you, as well.

Yet, despite all of these things, I'm still here. You're still here. That is no coincidence as far as I'm concerned. But it bothers me too, you know—that I'm still here, and they're not—the ones who had not the strength to go on. Or perhaps it wasn't strength, but rather, reason. Many of us can endure hardship and suffering. We may become bitter, resentful, and miserable because of it, but we can grit our teeth, clench our jaw, and press on—if we have something to press on toward. If we don't, then I guess the only question left to ask is, "What's the point in any of this?" I often find myself amazed at the tenacity of those who survived the concentration camps of Nazi Germany. To endure such grueling agonies, starvation, and torture—it is, in my estimation, nothing short of a miracle.

My first exposure to suicide came when I was in elementary school. A student, one grade ahead of me, had found his father hanged in his garage. At his young age, I'm not sure if his mind could compute what was before him. To this day, I still feel turmoil in my soul just thinking about it. I don't know the details surrounding the incident, or why his father had decided to do such a thing, but it makes no difference. A man with a family, for whatever reason, had lost hope, and his earthly story ended. He would never see his son grow up.

Other suicides happened around me throughout my life. In the past year or so, I've known of four local suicides. One, a woman who hanged herself outside on a tree, another, a man who shot himself behind a shopping mall in his car, and others, two young students who killed themselves. It's clear to me that suicide isn't something one can escape. It will always be around until Christ comes and redeems this fallen world.

I don't think that Scripture speaks much on the issue of suicide. We do read the narratives of those who commit it, such as King Saul, Abimelech, and Judas.[45] And even though Judas betrayed Christ, I still hate how his story ends. What it looks like to believe the lie that there is nothing left to live for. A lie, no surprise, that comes from the darkest depths.

At other times, there are those in the Bible who wish to die. Such are Moses, Elijah, Jonah, Jeremiah, Paul, and Job.[46] The Scriptures give some background and insight into these events, but it seems silent other than these mentions. However, the Bible does touch on suicide by its prohibition to murder—because that is what suicide is—self-murder. It is taking the authority over your life, in place of God, and doing what you want in opposition to what He commands. It's a matter, ultimately, of trust. Do we trust God to get us through our sufferings, that He has

[45] Their accounts are found in 1 Samuel 31:3–6, Judges 9:54, and Matthew 27:5, respectively. Add to the list Ahithophel (2nd Samuel 17:23) and Zimri (1 Kings 16:18).
[46] Numbers 11:14–15; 1st Kings 19:4; Jonah 1:12, 4:9; Jeremiah 20:14; Philippians 1:23; Job 3:11–19.

a plan, or do we renege on our convictions and take our own lives to escape it?

My suicidal depression, I must confess, confuses me at times. I grew up with two loving parents, had a roof over me, food in my mouth, and a pillow to lay my head upon at night. As far as I know, I hadn't suffered any sexual abuse, physical abuse, or traumatic event, unless those things preceded my ability to remember them. I had what I consider to be a positive childhood, yet despite this, I still struggled. Now, that is not to say that there was nothing bad in my life. That would have been a little easier. But no, like all of us, I tussled with the broken world around me.

Early on in my life, I felt the crippling weight of failure and insignificance. I have always lived in the shadow of an older brother who has excelled beyond me in almost everything (perhaps not the ability to grow facial hair—but I am sure he's not too remiss about that). Perhaps I could have dealt with that fine enough, but he was also awfully antagonistic and inflammatory, often serving as more of a tormentor than that of a brother. And even as young as we were, he could be quite relentless and uncannily creative in his ploys of belittlement. I, being the young man I was, of course did not outwardly show that his words were hurting me at deeper levels than he and I both probably assumed. What began as anger soon transitioned to nights of questioning myself, rehashing my failures, evaluating his successes, and wondering where I had gone wrong, and why I couldn't measure up to him. That was the bitter pill, the stinging injection. He was better than me, he knew it, and I could do nothing except cement my jaw shut to hide my gritting teeth. I was also the youngest, and we were relatively poor, so I got his hand-me-downs. That again, would have been tolerable—would have been—if he weren't several inches taller and tens of pounds heavier. And because he was the oldest, he often received first dibs on a lot of different things, leaving me behind in the dust.

The feeling of inadequacy, of not fitting in, of having my heart broken, and dashed expectations eventually piled up. I think about that from time to time. But somewhere along the way, my brain flipped a switch, and the lights went off. I didn't want to be here anymore. I felt useless, purposeless, vain—like I had to prove myself, but couldn't. An unattractive college drop-out with depression whose past was marked by failure and shame. Time and time again, I felt defeated. I'd perform poorly at work, jump from job to job due to becoming bored, have mini-existential crises about what I was going to do with the rest of my life. Pornography had hooks in my flesh. I didn't feel good about it.

This battle continued on and on. Even now, I can see the threads of my marionette leading to the ceiling with depression attempting to pull the strings because some things never leave you, no matter how hard you try to leave them. The strings fashioned to me feel like Prometheus's chains—unbreakable shackles that keep me prisoner while depression feeds upon my liver.[47] One example of this stems from my young adulthood. Growing up, I had always enjoyed writing. It was my passion. Well, I decided one day to write a story for my closest friends and brother. It was a fantasy work that centered on the imaginary characters we created for various games. What I thought would be a small project ended up becoming a story over two-hundred pages long. I was gushing proud and incredibly excited to have my close circle read it. I even made my brother's character, despite our shaky relationship, perform one of the more heroic deeds by felling the main villain. It was, in some way shape or form, me extending my hand to him in honor.

Only one of them read the work. The others gave little to no effort to do so. I even printed it out at my local Staples with the meager amount of money that I had, gifted it to one of them, only for him to discard it in place of another book which he cleaved through half of it in one night while my book sat in front of him. That was miserable but made worse by his gloating about how good the book he was currently reading was.

I lost all confidence to write. I sure as hell wasn't going to pursue authorship. That struck me as a bad joke. How could I justify becoming an author when those whom I wrote for and were closest to wouldn't even bother to read what I had written? How could I hope to think

---

[47] Prometheus was sentenced to eternal torment, shackled, and cursed to have a bird come and eat his liver every day after it grew back. The Greeks believed the liver to be the seat of human emotion.

that anyone else would read it? I didn't, so I stopped writing for a very long time.

That period of my life still hurts to reflect upon. I had poured myself into that book with all available energy and resource of mind. In a very real sense, that work was an extension of myself, a piece of me that was unique in the world, that could not be duplicated. It was something in which the mark of my creativity was indelibly stamped. And then there was the problem of not being able to get any of my girlfriends (the very few I had) to read it—strike two. I put it to rest before hitting strike three.

As you can glean, I eventually took up writing again. I wrote a book on relationships from a biblical perspective—and that has not been read by them, either. I'd be lying if I said it didn't hurt or remind me of what had happened before. But I'm older, wiser, and I recognize that all of us have to choose how we spend our time. No harm, no foul—we must continue marching on. I'm no fool, though. I feel the residual doubts about myself. When I try to share my works, it seems to be that not many persons take me seriously. It's somewhat frightening; am I engaging in futility by writing these works? Will anyone even read this one and come away feeling better about their depression and closer to God? Will this advance the kingdom at all? The Magic 8 Ball says, "Not a chance, kid," but I don't believe in chance. I believe in sovereignty, and if God wants to do a work using this book as His instrument, then to Him be the glory. His Word will not return void (Isaiah 55:11).

The continual sense of failure, rejection, and purposeless accelerated my depression. That's when the suicidal thoughts became rampant; easier to acknowledge and flirt with. That's when the gray inside your soul begins consoling you, persuading you that if you were gone, it would hurt those around you, but not too much. It certainly wouldn't be paradigm shifting. It would sting, it would bite, and it would bleed, but only for a moment. After that? Serenity and eyes forward because there's too much that goes on in life to stay in one place for too long.

After being in a place like that for any protracted period, you begin to lose hope. And once the well of hope becomes nothing more than vapors, you decide it's best to throw yourself to the bottom of the well instead of waiting to thirst to death. After all, the end result is the same, so why suffer until then when you've got two perfectly capable legs ready to spring?

These are the lies of sin, of death, of Satan. They're poison to the soul, war on the heart, and chaos in the mind. They're powerful agents, but they're not insurmountable. After all, I'm still here after fifteen years of assault—and I'm not that tough. So then, the strength I do have must come from somewhere or someone else. You are far enough in the book to realize where I'm taking you—back to the same cross that I've taken you to for the last several chapters.

For many of us, hope is nothing more than wishful thinking or whimsical desires for a better future that really has no basis in evidence, reason, or logic. In that manner, I hoped that Ken would survive his torn aorta. I had no medical justification for presuming he would—especially in light of the fact that his heart was functioning on 30% strength prior to the event—but nevertheless, I still hoped. That is the common understanding of hope, so that, when people see hope in the Bible, they read a modern understanding into the text that doesn't actually belong there.

When we speak of hope in the Bible, I suppose the easiest way to understand it (in my own mind) is to look at it as faith for the future. Faith is another word that receives a bad reputation due to the way people have categorized it. Faith is often qualified by the word blind: "You don't have evidence of God, you just have blind faith." As R.C. Sproul says, the idea most have of Christianity is that the Bible calls us to take a gratuitous leap of blind faith into the dark and hope we grab onto something while we're falling. Truth be told, the Bible nowhere calls us to blind faith, nor does it call us to blind hope. Faith in the Bible is equivalent to trust. We believe in the promises of God that affect us in the here and now—such as the promise of salvation for those who believe on the Lord Jesus Christ and repent of their sins. We have faith that Jesus Christ is God in the flesh, that the Bible is truly God's inerrant and infallible word given unto us, and that God is who He says He is. However, hope operates in the future. We set our hope on the future promises of God not yet realized. Hope in the new kingdom that God will usher in, where all things are made new, and sin is no more. Hope for glorified bodies, hope for rejoicing in God's immediate presence, hope for eternal life, and the list goes on. The idea of hope, then, is that it transports us from the present to better future things. This hope for future things then gives us a context in which the suffering we now experience can be meaningful, positive, and glorifying to God. It gives us the perspective to transcend the reality of earth to a greater reality of heaven. I know my time here is temporary, but I also know, because of the hope that I have in Christ, that I will also live forever in heaven with Him because of what He accomplished for me on the cross. Because I have hope (or future faith) in God, I have increased peace, increased security, and increased resilience because my God is sovereign over all, and He has given me the promise of life which supersedes all suffering—including my suicidal depression—now. Inwardly then, people also have this sense of hope. They hope for a better tomorrow, a good night's rest, a better time with their spouse, a possibility of promotion. They are banking on temporal things in a potential future to drive them forward, but what becomes of a man when the temporal hope he so heavily invested in comes crashing down around him? When the temporal reality crumbles, then there can be no temporal salvation. As Peter rightly says, everything perishes eventually (see 1 Peter 1:24). All of us then, whether we like it or not, whether we acknowledge it or not, know that we too, in this life, shall perish.

The idea of imminent perishing is the boogeyman in the closet that the world is too afraid to face head on. And if you're someone whose worldview dictates that there is nothing other than this life, then no wonder! Because if life has no continuity outside of these mortal frames we call bodies, then what is it that we're striving toward other than the proverbial cliff leading to our fatal plummet? This kind of worldview makes the surrounding reality all the more daunting. It makes it purposeless.

It's for this reason that I have often pondered how an atheist would respond if I told them that I struggle with the sort of depression that I do. Why should I continue to suffer when I can just put an end to all right now? What's the justification for living? Now, of course the answer would be that there's so much to live for and that others would be sad if I left, but in the final analysis, so what? They will die soon enough, perhaps even the day after I do, and if I choose to live, well then, there's one more straw on the back of the camel which was already broken ten straws ago. You see, the notion of having something to live for or toward is a nice sentiment, but it doesn't really answer the question of life as it correlates to suffering and the justification for being. What they are really trying to say is, "You've got some things here that you're attached to, that bring you modicums of joy, or sentimentality. Remember how your father used to take you to the park as a young boy with your brother? Remember how much you hated helping family move, but always looked forward to the inevitable pizza they'd buy for dinner, despite the fact that you'd only manage two to three slices of it when you really wanted eight? Don't those things keep your feet down here on earth? Don't they ground you?" Well, as pleasant as those things are, they don't exactly solve the dilemma. And that's not to say that those things are meaningless or lack weight, but rather, that the depression has tipped the scales in its favor and nothing you place on the other side can tip it back. Nothing can justify the pain.

Unless, perhaps, there's something or someone who can justify it, because as mysterious as it may seem, He has designed the world and your life and has ordered in such a way as to bring you to where you are. That's the mysterious tension between man's agency and God's sovereignty. It's the same tension we see in the book of Acts where Peter tells the Jews that they crucified Jesus according to the predestined plan of God (Acts 2:23–24). They hated Christ, had desires of murder, and carried them out, and yet they acted within the will of God's sovereignty because nothing escapes it. God did not force them to crucify Jesus, but it was part of God's plan. The thrust here, then, is that nothing occurring, including you reading this book, is out of the purview of God's sovereignty. And that's really quite beautiful to think about because on the one hand, there could be no God at all and all of your searching, and your toil, and your pain would be meaningless and without purpose. You would die, fade away, and it wouldn't have mattered. This is what drives the nihilist. If life could be over tomorrow, why be sober tonight? Why resist indulging in pleasures for the sake of appearances or some subjective moral code? The world is, in this worldview, survival of the fittest, and there are those who last a little longer, but none of us make it. We all die.

As you can see, the prospect of a godless universe is a bleak and hopeless one. Terrifying. Daunting. There are no good words to describe it. And if we are not careful, it's this kind of thinking that can drag us under dark waters and drown us.

When a man loses all sense of hope, when he tastes the bitter gall of despair, that is when the knife begins to look like a pillow—offering us the rest we so desperately crave. But the danger is in the deception of our minds because we're quite adept at painting pictures for ourselves that don't accord with reality. But depression does that. That is why we need to have a hope that goes beyond ourselves, one that can justify and contextualize our suffering, and provide the comfort and strength to fight against it.

One of my favorite Scriptures regarding this comes from the pen of the Apostle Paul. In 2nd Corinthians 1, Paul writes to the church in Corinth: **For we do not want you to be unaware, brothers, of the affliction we experienced in Asia. For we were so utterly burdened beyond our strength that we despaired of life itself. Indeed, we felt that we had received the sentence of death** (vv. 8–9a). Paul was intimately familiar with affliction. So much so, that one may be led to wonder how Paul retained his sanity. But not one to leave us in the dark, Paul elsewhere shares these afflictions with his audience:

Five times I received at the hands of the Jews the forty lashes less one. Three times I was beaten with rods. Once I was stoned.[48] Three times I was shipwrecked; a night and day I was adrift at sea; on frequent journeys, in danger from rivers, dangers from robbers, danger from my own people,

[48] The act of stoning a person involved either holding them down and striking their head with a large stone or burying them up to their necks and throwing stones at them with the desired outcome to kill them. See Acts 14:19–20.

danger from Gentiles, danger in the city, danger in the
wilderness, danger at sea, danger from false brothers; in
toil and hardship, through many a sleepless night, in hunger
and thirst, often without food, in cold and exposure. And,
apart from other things, there is the daily pressure on me of
my anxiety for all the churches. (2nd Corinthians 11:24–29)

Paul was also imprisoned for the gospel many times and the accounts of many of his trials can be found in the book of Acts. I think it is safe to say that Paul was not exaggerating when he said that he and his cohorts felt that they have received the sentence of the death, and there's a very important lesson to be learned from that kind of language.

Part of the reason why depression is so effective at deteriorating those who suffer it is because the widespread stigmatization of it. As mentioned before, if you confess that you suffer from depression, the reactions can be less than encouraging, if not downright demeaning. How much more so, then, for the problem of suicidal depression? If you think a person with depression is broken, then how do you describe someone whose depression has taken them to brink of self-destruction? So it is no easy feat to admit this, partly because those of us who do suffer it do not wish to admit it to ourselves. The external stigma becomes the internal stigma, too. This is a recipe for disaster as far as I'm concerned, and I've seen it play out in my life, bear hugging something to myself that I should have been pushing away and dealing with instead. That is why I find Paul's transparency on the matter so refreshing and at the same time, so radically different from what modern experience would have us believe about that transparency.

If we break this verse down and try to extract its essence, we can run off with much fruit that lends itself to the statements which Paul predicated this confession on, found in 2nd Corinthians 1:3–5: **Blessed be the God and Father of our Lord Jesus Christ, the Father of all mercies and God of all comfort, who comforts us in all our affliction, so that we may be able to comfort those who are in any affliction, with the comfort with which we ourselves are comforted by God. For as we share abundantly in Christ's sufferings, so through Christ we share abundantly in comfort too.**

Paul's openness has much utility because it humanizes Paul. We have the temptation to view the disciples and apostles of Christ in a superhuman light, but any good man of God knows from where his strength comes. Paul was human just like us, full of emotion, aspirations, disappointments, hurts, betrayals, questions, and sufferings. So in humility he opens up to his church. He lets them know in no uncertain terms that the work he's engaging in is costly, tedious, deadly. His willingness to sacrifice himself for it is a demonstration of how much it means to him to serve Christ and it validates the authenticity of his statement. He wants them to be aware of what he's going through for the gospel that he delivered to them.

We were so utterly burdened beyond our strength. That is quite a place to be. It's not yet quite in the chasm, but it's certainly not near the top of the well, either. It's a place of descent to a place of despair if one is not careful enough to escape it before it's too late. If Paul had left his statement as is above, there would still be hope. We all have run the gamut in some way, shape, or form. It's tough—a crucible of the will—but not insurmountable. As long as we can conceptualize of a future better than the meager sufferings of our present, we can generally draw additional, internal strength to combat the nefarious wiles of this cruel world. But Paul takes his statement further by adding, "that we despaired of life itself" (see 2nd Corinthians 1:8). That's not a statement to glance over dismissively—that is a weighty thing there. That is where the knife's edge is dangerous. To despair of circumstance or situation is one thing. I can despair of a wayward child who chases absurdity. I can despair of a marriage falling apart, or of a chronic health condition for myself or a loved one. I can despair of one thing, or a couple things, without being driven to the edge, because I can still recognize that the parts (the things I despair over) are distinct from the whole (life itself). While I may be amiss that my apple tree is producing some rather unsightly apples, I can still enjoy the sweetness of those apples whose flavor has yet to be soured.

In other words, I'm not swinging my ax at the root of the tree because there is still fruit being produced that is worthy of protecting, nourishing, and investing in. The tree is still producing something positive, but in Paul's case, the entire tree is despaired of because everything it is producing is attended by the stench and taste of death. In that instance, you not only ax the cursed tree, but you burn it altogether and rue its existence. Nothing should remain of that, much like the symbolic branches that do not remain in Christ are tossed into the fire (see John 15:6). When your life is despaired of as a whole, then you are in the chasm of unplumbed depths. And what is one to do in a situation like that? We already know the tragic answer because we have seen this kind of scenario play out time and time again.

Just because you're burdened beyond your strength doesn't mean that it has to be the end. A loose analogy comes from my childhood. I lived in a house with a basement in which my father kept two things: his woodworking equipment and his old-school weightlifting equipment. One day, while my father was downstairs working on his carpentry projects, I decided to go under the bar on the bench press and test my mettle. I lifted the weightless bar, brought it down to my chest, and pressed it up. No problem. I added some more weight. Nothing too much, but still, something that could challenge my body. Maybe something along the lines of sixty-five pounds. Keep in mind, I was a kid, not an Olympic power lifter.

I continued to progress until I reached ninety-five pounds, and I think that I was excited because now I had two twenty-five-pound plates on the bar and that was like the next step in the weightlifting world (increasing a plate size). I thought to myself, "Well, eighty-five was tough, but it wasn't all that tough. I can bench ninety-five pounds." Well, I was wrong. That bar dropped down to my chest, I squeaked it up about an inch or so, and then it fell back upon my tiny frame like a hammer. I started calling out to my father who had his back turned to me. He didn't turn around. I called out to him as loudly as I could, but to no avail. He wasn't wearing ear plugs or playing loud music. He wasn't doing anything of the sort because my father is deaf. He had no idea that his flailing, thin, and foolish son was calling out to him, pinned under a meager ninety-five pounds. Eventually my father did turn around. He rolled his eyes and shook his head and signed "dumb" at me (which involves knocking your fist against your forehead twice) before walking over and effortlessly hoisting the weight from my chest and back onto the rack. At that moment, with the ninety-five pounds lying across my chest, I was burdened beyond my own strength, but I wasn't out of the fight. Looking back on the ninety-five-pound dilemma, I chuckle because ninety-five pounds seemed like a lot of weight, and it was, but only relative to my size and strength at that time. The weakness suffered then is not the weakness suffered now, and what burdens us today may not necessarily burden us tomorrow. But the saving grace, whether for the present or the future, has to be something that grants us strength beyond ourselves and what it is that burdens us. For me in the basement, it was the superior strength of my father and his willingness to help that saved the day, and his being present with me in the basement. Let me say it again: my father had to have the strength necessary to save me, he had to possess the willingness to save me, and he had to be present with me to save me. All of those elements needed to be in place before any saving could happen, and they had to be in place simultaneously. What I am trying to say is that if you are feeling burdened beyond your strength right now, that doesn't mean that it's time to throw in the towel. You're still here—that's got to count for something—but you need to look beyond yourself for salvation. Paul doesn't stop there. He continues on and says, **Indeed, we felt that we had received the sentence of death** (2nd Corinthians 1:9a). The burden of his trials, the despair of life itself—those things culminated into feeling as though the end was nigh. If you've struggled the same way in which I have, then you have probably experienced the "sentence of death" sensation that Paul here details, the feeling of being inside a collapsing world. Strong as you may be, you can't stave off death and no matter how long and hard you train, you won't be bench-pressing open your casket anytime soon.

The key word in Paul's declaration here is felt. To feel something is in a sense, to interpret reality, and this can be somewhat relative depending on the person. What may feel like a sentence of death on me may be laughable from the perspective of another and vice versa. Fair. But we also know that our emotions are communicating to us about our external reality, too. I get angry at an event. The anger is communicating on some level that I have been wronged. It doesn't mean it's an accurate estimation of the actual event, but it's a perceived one, nonetheless. So if I feel as though I have received the sentence of death, I don't think there can be a bleaker outlook on what's transpiring in my life to make me feel that way. Because of this, when we look over Paul's statement here, we can see that his confession has multiple layers to it that build upon each other, expressing the weight of his situation. What can we do in such a miserable estate?

But that was to make us rely not on ourselves but on God who raises the dead (2nd Corinthians 1:9b). Here Paul lays out the utility of burden. Recall that man's purpose in life is fellowship with God, worshiping Him, and enjoying Him forever. Part of that purpose is a continual recognition of who God is in contrast to us, and from that recognition, a continual dependence on Him. This should not come as a surprise since we only exist by the will and power of God sustaining us (see Hebrews 1:3). If Paul's statement is true, then it would seem to indicate that God's will was for Paul and his companions to endure trials and tribulations to remind them of their dependence on God. At first take, this may seem cruel—why would God will for these events to be? Well, what's the alternative? If Paul and his companions rely upon their own strength, by their own admission, they aren't going to last very long. That's not a good thing—not for Paul and his friends, nor the Corinthian church—least of all not good for us seeing how Paul penned more than half the New Testament. So what's worse? Relying on yourself when you know that you are weak, brittle, and easily defeated? Or relying on God whose very name is strong tower and place of refuge?[49] And is it not true that sometimes we have to let those that we love endure trial and tribulation so that they might learn an invaluable lesson that words alone could not teach to the same degree? Paul could have relied on himself, or he could have relied on God. One was a source of meager and fleeting strength, and the other was a fount of endless strength. Which one do you think Paul would choose?

I've already mentioned in passing that I've prayed to God to grant me

---

[49] Proverbs 18:10 says, "The name of the LORD is a strong tower; the righteous man runs into it and is safe."

the strength to keep going. But I left out the details. I don't remember all of them, but I recall a good amount of them—good enough to share.

At that time, a few years prior to this work, I was pacing in my studio apartment. It was nighttime, and I was feeling an incredible weight, somewhere within me, perhaps in the stomach, but deeper if you can imagine that. I think I had experienced another heartache with another girl. That was probably it. Most people would look at that, roll their eyes, and think, "Get over it," and that's perfectly sound advice for a reasonable person, but when you're contemplating suicide, reasonableness has already left the party. So the repetitive thought of my romantic failure was more like a resounding hammer, incessantly striking me where I was most prone to break. It was prone because my entire life had been a muddled mess of romantic gaffes. I was a hopeful, naïve, and somewhat misguided Romeo. I was low in confidence, easily provoked to comparison with other men, highly jealous, and not comfortable in my own skin. So maybe not so much like Romeo, after all.

In any case, I was in despair. I was thinking of every failure of my life, how I hated the idea of becoming attached to someone only to have them rip themselves away. It hurt. I felt as though I really wasn't good enough or else, why would they give up on me? Or perhaps, the question also was, "Why didn't they give me a chance?" Outwardly I had the appearance of a young man, but inwardly, I felt like a lost child, sitting by himself in the alleyway under a gray sky and cold rains, watching the legs of people much bigger than me pass me by in a crowd—a blur—wondering if they even saw me at all. Wondering if this little boy was gone today, would anyone notice tomorrow? I felt overlooked. Insignificant. Purposeless. My childhood experiences reinforcing those feelings certainly didn't help.

I was isolated and trapped within my own mind. To try to not think about suicide led me to think about suicide. I didn't have anyone I could turn to or reach out to because nobody knew what I struggled with. I was partially ashamed of my weakness and partially still in self-denial. My reliance on my own strength was a fool's errand.

Well, it wasn't long before the world came crashing down around me and the whispers became roars. I began to sweat, and then my eyes began to well. I choked up. I wanted to grab a knife. I fought that temptation, as beautiful as it appeared at the moment promising me sweet release, I fought with all of my fleeting strength. It wasn't enough, though, because the temptation grew astonishingly strong. And I was deathly afraid because this was the strongest that it had ever been before—I could feel the switch wanting to flip off and knew that if it did—game over. The clock was ticking. Each second that passed felt like agony. I saw the hall to freedom stretching out before me, its length too great to conquer. I was frozen, thoughts frantic, under the dull ambient sounds of a low-budget studio apartment.

I ran to my bed and dropped to my knees and began praying the same prayer out loud over and over: "Please, God, don't let me kill myself." He didn't. God gave me strength, clarity, and courage. I reached out to my boss who was also a very dear friend and I told him. And shortly after that, I began to open up, layer by layer, eventually telling my brother, my mother, and my father. Some of my friends. My soon to be girlfriend who then became my wife. And at that moment, I experienced, I believe, in part, what Paul did: **[God] delivered us from such a deadly peril, and He will deliver us. On Him we have set our hope that He will deliver us again** (2nd Corinthians 1:10). What a powerful statement!

What makes this statement so powerful is that if read correctly, it shows the faithfulness of God. Why do I say this? Well, read the text again. Did you notice anything? A pattern of sorts? What Paul says is that (1) God delivered, (2) God will deliver, and (3) God will deliver again. What Paul is emphasizing here is a triple-tense deliverance of past, present, and future action. God delivered them before; God is delivering them currently; and God will deliver them again in the future; a trinity of deliverance. Paul learned reliance on God, and this reliance translated to a hope set on the power and goodness of God! And why could Paul trust this? Because as he had already said in verse nine, God is one who can raise the dead! And to take it further, God is the one who delivers us from death every breath we take! So the God who delivered Paul and me in the past is the same God who can deliver you in the present and the future! And through this we can see just how it is that Paul called God the "God of all comfort" and how Paul's sufferings enabled him to comfort the Corinthian church. We are much more adept at comforting others if we've experienced the travails of their souls. And in this way, our old cries in the night become our new song in the day to bring hope to those who feel they've received the sentence of death—to those who despair of life itself. And if you need any further evidence that Paul's words strike true, then look at the book you are reading. If I did not struggle with depression and suicidal depression at that, I'd have nothing here to offer you. To be sure, greater books on this issue exist—they have to—but those books can't detail and outline my experience. Only I can do that because my experience is unique, and so is yours. You have a voice, a testimony, a sword to cut through the lies of Satan and chaos—if you so choose to pick it up. And what is this sword that grants you its sharp edge? **For the word of God is living and active, sharper than any two-edged sword, piercing to the division of soul and of spirit, of joints and of marrow, and discerning the thoughts and intentions of the heart** (Hebrews 4:12).

The truth is, if you are fighting this battle, it is easy to get overwhelmed. But if you know the promises of God, lean on Him, and see through the veil of suicide's deception, then there is an immovable hope, and His name is Jesus Christ, the Word of God. He is a God of life, not death—of peace and grace. He calls you to Himself, to trust Him in all things, and to leave behind the shackles of death which so ensnare you. It doesn't mean that all of your troubles go away. I love you too much to lie to you. Even I still battle with my depression, but the fight is easier because I know Who is in my corner. Woes still continue to exist in my life—those don't go away—but they can be dealt with in a manner that is responsible and meaningful. My perspective has been helped by God, and if God can do it for me, assuredly, He can do it for you, if you have faith. We can know from where our help comes.

Don't run without hope. Don't tread the treacherous and dark waters. Take it from me that if you're still breathing and you're still here, then there is still light for you.

Like I had said before, if you do feel the desire to hurt yourself, there is nothing wrong acknowledging that and moving toward others who can help you in your fight. If you are a believer, that doesn't mean that you cannot seek counseling and guidance. If you do not know Christ, my encouragement is to seek Him while He still may be found, but also to seek counseling and guidance from professionals who know the mind—and preferably those who know Christ. Churches generally offer their counseling for free as far as I know. The suicide prevention organization can also provide you resources and an ear to talk to if things get to be too much.[50]

As a brief aside, I wanted to share a story from a woman who attends my local church because I think it paints a powerful picture of how one can be redeemed from the proverbial cliff's edge. This woman in my church had struggled in an abusive relationship, got into drugs, and was living a life spiraling out of control. To make matters worse, she had two young kids. Boys, I think. As her life continued to degrade, she found herself becoming more and more despondent, left without answers, and running low on any sort of hope. She didn't know Christ. One day, she received a letter in the mail from a friend that was personally delivered to her door. The delivery of this letter came seconds before she was about to murder her children and then kill herself, having felt that she had nothing left to live for.

Deciding to read the letter before committing her atrocious deed, she soon discovered that the letter was from an old friend who was a believer in Christ. In this letter, he expressed his desire to see her know Christ, to find hope in Him, and outlined the great love that Jesus displayed and offers through the cross where He died to save sinners once and for all. She broke down, repented of her sins, placed her faith in Christ, and God did a mighty work in her, saving not only her and her sons' lives, but more importantly, their souls. This letter came within seconds of a woman who felt she had no other answer to her dilemma than death, and it instead led to life. The work of the Lord is truly mysterious.

Unfortunately, not every story ends this way. For some, no letter is delivered, and the irrevocable choice is made. Many people have asked,

---

[50] The National Suicide Prevention Lifeline number is 1-800-273-8255.

"What happens to a person if they commit suicide? Can that sin be forgiven or is it the ultimate sin that leads to eternal damnation?"

When I was a young boy, I had this debate with my friends. I remember standing next to the fridge and discussing it. Even in my youth, I think I had enough sense to deny such a claim. The reason I deny it, and I think I have a biblical warrant to do so, is because when Christ died on the cross for those who would believe on His name, He paid for all their sins, the sin of suicide included. While suicide is self-murder and is a tragic occurrence, it is not an unforgivable one. It is one that should never be sought after, but it is possible for Christians to experience such grief and lack of sober-mindedness that they succumb to thoughts or circumstances and take their own lives. And such who do will be welcomed into the arms of their Savior because their sins were paid for in full. To be clear, a person is condemned to hell because they bear the weight, responsibility, and guilt of their sins before a holy and righteous God. But for those who trust in Jesus, Christ has paid their debt in their place for them, and thus no penalty for sin remains.

Your life has meaning. Your life has purpose. And your life has hope. His name is Jesus, and His arms are always open, ready to receive any who come to Him. It is my sincere desire that this chapter in some way, shape, or form has helped you. I pray it is so! You are not alone, so even when it gets dark, when the world feels as though it's too cruel, too vast, too gray...

Don't close the curtain.

9

But Upon Seeing the Flower, I Knew

Up until this point, we have labored extensively to go over depression, suffering, and the myriad of ailments that plague the human race. We have, with all genuine effort, attempted to answer the problem of depression in its various manifestations and causes. We avoided providing the unrealistic expectation that believing in Jesus means that all bad feelings and events cease to be from your life from that point forward, and we also shared wisdom on how to combat depression when it arises.

As stated in the first chapter of this book, my main goal was to constantly point you, the reader, to Christ. That is where you will find healing for every wound because when Christ redeemed us on the cross, He redeemed the totality of who we are—body, mind, and soul. We still have to live out our experience here under the tumults of life, but we do so knowing that Christ has redeemed all of us, even our depression.

It took me a long time to realize that the Lord was using my depression to mold me into the man that He needed me to be. I remember talking with another Christian couple who told me that they didn't believe it was God's will for me to suffer from my depression. I adamantly disagreed. They meant well, and I understood what they were trying to say—that pain and suffering was not what God wanted for me—but still, I disagreed. I believe that my depression was something God had given unto me to steward.

This point is captured in David Murray's book, *Christians Get Depressed Too*. On page eight, Dr. Murray writes,

> *"Like all affliction in the lives of Christians, depression should be viewed as a talent[51] (Matt. 25:14–30) that can be invested in such a way that it brings benefit to us and others as well as glory to God. Christian psychologist James Dobson observed, "Nothing is wasted in God's economy." That "nothing" includes depression."*

On the next page, Dr. Murray shares a powerful quote from Ruth Stull of Peru: "If my life is broken when given to Jesus, it is because pieces will feed a multitude, while a loaf will satisfy only a little lad."

I share Ruth Stull's sentiment. How can Christians comfort others if they themselves have not been comforted in their own sufferings? How can Christians testify to the goodness of God if they do not walk in the valley of the shadow of death? How can those who have never been hopeless appreciate and share the hope of the gospel? How can a Christian write a book about his depression for the sake of others if he has never himself been depressed?

I would gladly shatter into thousands of pieces if it meant that I could help others in their pain and weakness. Because I know that Jesus has me in the safety of His hands and can never lose me (John 10:28) my suffering then becomes a resource for others who share the same plight. I believe in this firmly because it is what Jesus models for us in the gospels.

---

[51] A "talent" in this context does not refer to a unique ability, but rather, a currency.

A MAN OF SORROWS

Those unfamiliar with the life of Jesus may be under the false assumption that Jesus lived a posh life with no turbulence. However, the picture that the Scriptures paint regarding the life of Jesus is far less flattering than one might think. Jesus's entire life was marked out by suffering and trials, prophesied even before His birth. Then, during His infancy, He was already under assault by the vicious edict of king Herod, who ordered that every baby ages two and under be executed. Jesus was born in a manger, surrounded by filth and manure and animals—born into poverty. When His ministry began, He often faced ridicule and persecution from the leaders of the Jews. God in the flesh suffered rejection and loss. Listen to the prophecy of Isaiah concerning the Christ and compare it to John's testimony of Him:

> *He was despised and rejected by men, a man of sorrows and acquainted with grief; and as one from whom men hide their faces He was despised, and we esteemed Him not. Surely He has borne our griefs and carried our sorrows; yet we esteemed Him stricken, smitten by God, and afflicted. But He was pierced for our transgressions; He was crushed for our iniquities; upon Him was the chastisement that brought us peace, and with His wounds we are healed.* (Isaiah 53:4–6)

> *The true light, which gives light to everyone, was coming into the world. He was in the world, and the world was made through Him, yet the world did not know Him. He came to His own, and His own people did not receive Him.* (John 1:9–11)

Jesus is called the "man of sorrows" who is "acquainted with grief" and as one whom "men hide their faces." This prophecy is accurate. Jesus, by all accounts, was not the Messiah that the Jews had anticipated. They wanted a war king and Jesus came as the servant king. He came as a lamb when the Jews wanted a devouring lion. Jesus came to redeem them from the bondage of sin, but they wanted redemption from the bondage of Rome. They were the spiritually blind leading the blind.

This is not to say that many were not awestruck by Jesus's miracles. Certainly, Jesus had a large following at times of people wanting to see signs and miracles. In other words, many of Jesus's followers were just there for a show. When Jesus began to teach hard sayings, the crowds would disperse: **After this Jesus went away to the other side of the Sea of Galilee, which is the Sea of Tiberias. And a large crowd was following Him, because they saw the signs that He was doing on the sick.... And [Jesus] said, "This is why I told you that no one can come to Me unless it is granted him by the Father." After this many of His disciples turned back and no longer walked with Him. So Jesus said to the twelve, "Do you want to go away as well?"** (John 6:1–2, 65–67). In other words, Jesus was just an object of the peoples' entertainment. They did not follow Him for the right reasons. And even when Jesus performed miracles, such as raising Lazarus from the dead, there were those who did not believe: **Many of the Jews therefore, who had come with Mary and had seen what [Jesus] did, believed in Him, but some of them went to the Pharisees and told them what Jesus had done** (John 11:45–46). The Pharisees wanted a reason to put Jesus away for good. Despite having seen Jesus raise Lazarus from his tomb, some Jews left to report Jesus to the Pharisees instead of believing in Him on account of His works. Jesus was constantly rejected by His people (Mark 6:4) and was doubted even by His own family (John 7:5)! Indeed, the world hated Jesus (v. 7).

It is in this kind of setting—a place of poverty[52] and without honor—that the Son came to reconcile sinners to Himself. To be despised, rejected, persecuted, and eventually crucified. But it was not the crucifixion that concerned Jesus—though there was much pain to be wrought in the piercing of flesh—but it was rather drinking the cup of the Father's wrath to the last drop. For Christ to atone for those

---

[52] Matthew 8:20 records Jesus's statement for us regarding His poverty. Jesus says, "Foxes have holes and birds of the air have nests, but the Son of Man has no place to lay His head." Jesus was often destitute. When the tax collectors came to obtain taxes from Jesus, Jesus instructed Peter to obtain the tax from the fish of a mouth (Matthew 17:24–27).

who would believe in Him, He would have to go to the cross, a place of humiliating death for the worst of criminals and die there. But part of this transaction was bearing the full weight of God's wrath upon Himself in our place, paying the eternal debt of hell that we could never pay off. Paul says that Christ became sin for us and nailed our transgressions to the cross.[53] This event that changed the history of the world forever had such a weight to it, that prior to its occurrence, Christ agonized to the point of sweating drops of blood (Luke 22:44).[54] He even prayed twice to the Father to pass this cup of wrath from Him, if it were possible to do so. Why would Jesus ask this? Because, as He shared with His disciples, **"My soul is overwhelmed with sorrow to the point of death"** (see Matthew 26:38; Mark 14:34).

We miss this in today's evangelicalism. We so severely undercut the wrath of God in our sermons that to even mention God's hatred of sin or righteous judgment against the impenitent is to be viewed as a brimstone and fire preacher. Yet, if we are to worship God, should we not worship all of Him? Of course. This also means, then, that we need to *share* all of Him, especially in light of the fact that when we share the gospel of Christ, we are sharing the way unto salvation. To obtain salvation from something is to be saved from it. Well, what is God saving us from in Jesus? Himself. His wrath. His righteous indignation. When we speak of these attributes of God, we are telling people that they are not inherently righteous nor good. They are not worthy of God's love. They only deserve condemnation because God is holy, and they are not. The descriptions of God's wrath are by no means pleasant, nor do they pull their punches. In his book, *Saved From What?* R.C. Sproul quotes an Old Testament passage from the prophet Zephaniah to stress just how terrifying the wrath of God truly is. He quotes:

> *The great day of the LORD is near,*
> *near and hastening fast;*
> *the sound of the day of the LORD is*

---

[53] Colossians 2:14.

[54] This is a reference to a rare medical condition called hematidrosis, that causes sweat to contain blood. The known cause is such extreme anguish as to rupture the tiny blood vessels that surround the sweat glands.

bitter;
the mighty man cries aloud there.
A day of wrath is that day,
a day of distress and anguish,
a day of ruin and devastation,
a day of darkness and gloom,
a day of clouds and thick darkness,
a day of trumpet blast and battle cry
against the fortified cities
and against the lofty battlements.

I will bring distress on mankind,
so that they shall walk like the blind,
because they have sinned against the
LORD;
their blood shall be poured out like
dust,
and their flesh like dung.
Neither their silver nor their gold
shall be able to deliver them
on the day of the wrath of the LORD.
In the fire of His jealousy,
all the earth shall be consumed;
for a full and sudden end
He will make of all the inhabitants of
the earth. (Zephaniah 1:14–18)

When we comprehend the holy nature of God and the righteousness of God, and when we grip the extensive weight of God's wrath against sin, then that's when we realize that Jesus experienced suffering in ways that we will never comprehend. The supernatural phenomena experienced on the cross of Calvary, the weight of eternal judgment, the wrath of God—who could ever probe such mystery? And Jesus knew all of this was to come. His ministry, His very existence, was predicated on this mission.[55] In fact, when Jesus told His disciples that He must go and die, Peter pulls Jesus aside and privately rebukes Him (Matthew 16:22)! Jesus tells Peter, **"Get behind Me, Satan! You are a hindrance to me. For you are not setting your mind on the things of God, but on the things of man"** (v. 23). To try to stop the work of the cross was to do the work of Satan because it was only by way of the cross that salvation could come to fallen sinners, an event Satan desperately wanted to stop.

When we look at Jesus's life as one marked out by distinct and unique sufferings, we can hardly make the claim that Jesus does not understand our sorrows or trials, or that suffering had no utility in the life of Christ when Scripture makes it clear that it did: **For we do not have a high priest who is unable to sympathize with our weaknesses, but we have one who was tempted in every way that we are, yet without sin** (Hebrews 4:15), and, **Although [Jesus] was a son, He learned obedience through what He suffered** (Hebrews 5:8).

Our Lord can identify with us in our weakness because He took on human flesh and was beset with the same frailties of human experience as us. He experienced hunger, thirst, sorrow, pain, grief, and betrayal. He knew abandonment. He knew what it was to be scourged, ridiculed, and persecuted, but He knew the surpassing worth of knowing the Father and the Spirit. At the end of the day, our relationship with God is all that matters. All other distractions in this world are not worth mentioning in light of the Lord's redemption offered through Jesus.

I long for the day when I can put depression, sin, and death far behind me. I look toward the future eternity spent with Christ in perfect peace. Like Paul, I have a desire to be at home with the Lord, but also know that while I am still here breathing, God has work for me to do. And it's the same for you, beloved: **He who began a good work in you will carry it out on to completion until the day of Christ Jesus** (Philippians 1:6). And why did Paul desire to be at home with the Lord? **Because I consider that the sufferings of this present time are not worth comparing with the glory that is to be revealed to us** (Romans

---

[55] In Luke 9:22, Jesus says, "The Son of Man must suffer many things and be rejected by the elders, and chief priests, and scribes, and He must be killed and on the third day be raised to life."

8:18). When that day comes, we will receive new, resurrected bodies in Christ by His Spirit (1 Corinthians 15:35–49) free of depression, pain, and agony. No more feelings of loneliness. No more feelings of inadequacy or of wondering, or of purposelessness. No more tears on our pillows. No more heartbreaks, no more death, no more loss, no more lies, no more crime, no more sickness, no more despair. When we arrive at that day, ushered into our Savior, oh, what a joy it will be! A place where all things are made new. It's the great promises of Scripture that take me back to my days with Ken, who often looked forward to the day he would be with his Lord in glory. In fact, when we were at Ken's funeral, we sang three of his favorite hymns. One of them was called *When We All Get to Heaven* by Eliza K. Hewitt and Eliza D. Wilson. The song has a very "uppity" tune to it, full of swells of joyous emotions and celebrations. No matter how bad my day was going, whenever we sang this song, it was hard not to feel a burst of life enter the soul.

That is what we need, those of us who suffer from depression. We need new life, the kind of life that God offers us through Jesus: **But if Christ is in you, although the body is dead because of sin, the Spirit is life because of righteousness. If the Spirit of Him who raised Jesus from the dead dwells in you, He who raised Christ Jesus from the dead will also give life to your mortal bodies through His Spirit who dwells in you** (Romans 8:10–11).

I looked out the window after the storm, and I saw the flower. I saw what grew as a result of the rain. I saw what had to be, for something to become. It was then that I understood that the depression I've suffered with for over half my life was no longer something to mourn over, but something to rejoice in, for by it, God had made me the man I am today, and in this light, I am free.

You can be too.

Printed in the United States
by Baker & Taylor Publisher Services